Gardens to Visit
2006

Publicity Works

P.O. Box 32

Tetbury

Gloucestershire

GL8 8BF

© Tony Russell

Gardens to Visit 2006

Welcome to Gardens To Visit 2006. I really cannot believe that a full year has passed since I sat down to write the introduction to the 2005 edition and yet here we are at the end of another season of garden visits!

May I first of all say thank you for the hundreds of letters I have received – both from garden owners and from garden visitors – telling me just how helpful Gardens To Visit has been for those of you organising visits to gardens right across the UK. In general terms it would appear, from the feedback we have received, that more visits were made to gardens in 2005 than in the previous year – which is very encouraging.

I am delighted to be able to tell you that once again we have increased the overall number of gardens featured within Gardens To Visit. This year you will find 40 new and exciting gardens for you to explore – alongside, of course, your tried and tested favourites. Each garden has its own full colour page which includes a beautiful photograph, a 140 word description detailing the main features of the garden and a fact file which provides all the very latest information you need when planning a visit.

Within Gardens To Visit 2006 there are gardens to suit all tastes, from old favourites such as Abbey House Gardens, Savill Gardens and Stourhead, to some very beautiful but perhaps less well known gardens such as Cerney House, Upton House and the delightful Cornish gardens of Penjerrick.

Also, for the first time in this publication, we are offering readers the opportunity to join one of our special Gardens To Visit Tours. For 2006 I shall be leading tours to the beautiful 'floral island' of Jersey. Over five days, in both spring and summer, we shall be exploring some of the amazing horticultural diversity which is to be found in this southern-most island of the British Isles.

I do hope you enjoy this brand new collection of gardens and may I wish you a very successful and enjoyable season of garden outings in 2006.

Tony Russell BBC garden writer and broadcaster.

Opposite: Holker Hall, Cumbria. See page 40.

Visit Some of the most Beautiful
Gardens in Jersey

'The Garden Isle of the British Isles'
In the company of the BBC Garden Writer and
Broadcaster **Tony Russell**

Jersey is the most southerly of the Channel Islands and has one of the best sunshine records in the British Isles. It is 100 miles south of mainland Britain and 14 miles from the coast of France.

Jersey is a plant paradise. A mild climate and fertile soil makes it possible to grow an astonishing range of trees, shrubs and flowers. Part of the thrill of gardening in Jersey is the sheer speed at which plants grow, faster by far than anywhere else in the British Isles. The island's unique climate and topography means sub-tropical plants thrive in gardens facing the sea and in south-facing sites basking in sun from morning to evening. As such, special and beautiful gardens abound in Jersey – many in protected valleys and on slopes running down to sheltered coves and sandy bays.

This exclusive tour, will visit some of the finest gardens that Jersey has to offer – including some which rarely open their gates to the general public. From the romantic crumbling ruins of the Victorian Sub-tropical Gardens of La Chaire to the magical gardens created over the last twenty years by Judith Queree (BBC Gardener of the Year Competition 2001) this tour will cover almost two hundred years of Jersey's horticultural heritage.

Tours will take place in spring and summer 2006. These are five day, four night tours, with nights being spent in the beautiful Highfield Country Hotel.

The cost is just £549.00 per person and this includes all flights, coaches, accommodation and food.

Interested? Then contact David Lord at the Highfield Country Hotel
Telephone 01534 862194 – for more details.

Contents

England

" We met at a tea-table, the silver kettle and the conversation reflecting rhododendrons".

Sir Edwin Lutyens

So what is an English garden? Well as you explore these pages you will begin to see

that such is the diversity and individuality of English gardens, that to capture in one sentence

the typical English garden is virtually impossible. It is like attempting to capture in a bottle,

the sweet mixed fragrance of Philadelphus and rose after the rain has ceased on a

warm June evening.

Be it the garden or the fragrance, enjoy them

as you can and commit their charm to memory.

Opposite: Ragley Hall, Warwickshire. See page 147.

The Swiss Garden was created in the early nineteenth century. It contains picturesque features hidden in an undulating nine-acre landscape. The garden is planted with magnificent trees and ornamental shrubs which are arranged in a series of glades, lawns and winding walks, designed to provide unexpected vistas. The recently refurbished and replanted, subterranean grotto and fernery nestles in the centre. 'The Grand Tour' provided inspiration for the tiny thatched Swiss Cottage. The fashion for 'Swiss" architecture, so popular in the Regency period can be seen all around the Garden. Elegant floral arches and a network of ponds with decorative bridges and delightful islands complete the picture. Peafowl roam freely in the garden. Spring bulbs, rhododendrons and rambling roses are spectacular in season. Benches are located at frequent intervals. There is also an adjacent picnic area and a woodland lakeside walk.

Fact File

Opening Times: November 1st to March 31st 10am - 4pm, April 1st to October 31st 10am - 5pm

Admission Rates: Adults £4.00, Senior Citizen £3.00, Child Free.

Group Rates: Minimum group size: 20 but all groups welcome
Adults £3.50, Senior Citizen £2.50, Child Free.

Facilities: Visitor Centre, Restaurant, Toilets, Gift/Souvenirs and Plant Stall.

Disabled Access: Yes, Toilet and parking for disabled on site. Wheelchairs on loan, booking advised.

Tours/Events: Guided Tours and Group Bookings by appointment.

Coach Parking: Yes.

Length of Visit: 2 hours

Booking Contact: Karen Wilsher
The Swiss Garden, Old Warden Park, Old Warden, Biggleswade, Bedfordshire, SG18 9EP.
Telephone: 01767 627924 Fax: 01767 627949

Email: karen.wilsher@shuttleworth.org

Website: www.shuttleworth.org

Location: Approximately 2 miles west of Biggleswade A1 roundabout signposted from A1 and A600.

Please quote this guide when booking

We try to maintain the gardens to high standards but to allow the shrubs and plants to grow, flower and seed in abundance.

The pleached lime walk runs through the enormous herbaceous borders, which display an exuberance of scillas and alliums early on followed by mixed planting with the whole length edged with hostas of many different types.

The walled garden has a dramatic amount of blue and white delphiniums with earlier a great display of peonies.

The rose garden is yellow and white with some blue. The groundcover of violas has spread in sheets. A stream flow through which feeds the ponds and the fountain.

A very extensive herb garden lies near the greenhouses and beyond this is the wildflower meadow.

A large wood with two lakes makes a wonderful extension to the garden and excellent for walking the dog (and owner!)

Fact File

Opening Times:	Open only for groups, except Monday 29th May (Bank Holiday).
Admission Rates:	(on 29th May) Adults: £3.50 Senior Citizens: £3.50, Children: Free
Group Rates:	Minimum Groups Size: 20
	Adults/Senior Citizens: £5.00
Facilities:	Teas/coffee and homemade biscuits for groups.
Disabled Access:	Yes – part. Toilet and car parking on site.
Tours/Events:	Guided tours available.
Coach Parking:	Yes
Length of Visit:	2 hours
Booking Contact	Lady Bowman-Shaw
	Toddington Manor, Toddington Bedfordshire LU5 6HJ
	Telephone: 01525 872576 Fax: 01525 874555
Email:	None
Website:	www.toddingtonmanor.co.uk
Location:	1 mile from Junction 12, M1 motorway

Please quote this guide when booking

There are magnificent views from the nine acre garden at Englefield over the lake to the Kennet valley and the wooded ridge beyond.

The woodland and water garden, designed and planted by Wallace and Barr in the 1930's, has a canopy of ancient forest trees underplanted with a wide variety of shrubs and trees including acer, cornus, camellia, magnolia, azalea, davidia and rhododendron. A grotto has lately been built at the top of the stream, lined with a mosaic of varieties of pine cone.

The grey stone balustrades and wide staircases, built in 1860, enclose the lower terraces with their formal planting of mixed roses, topiary, wide lawns and water features. There are small enclosed areas, some lately paved and pebbled, and a children's garden with hidden jets off water from four small statues.

Fact File

Opening Times: Monday throughout the Year.
Monday, Tuesday, Wednesday, Thursday 1st April to 1st November 10am to 6pm.

Admission Rates: Adults £3.00, Children free.

Facilities: Plant Sales at Englefield Garden Centre (100 yards), Refreshments at Village Tea Room (100-150 yards).

Disabled Access: Yes - Limited.

Tours/Events: Guided tours for groups.

Coach Parking: Yes.

Length of Visit: 1 hour minimum.

Booking Contact: Mrs Gloria Sleep.
Englefield House, Englefield, Reading, Berkshire, RG7 5EN
Telephone: 0118 9302221 Fax: 0118 9303226

Email: gloria@englefield.co.uk

Website: www.englefield.co.uk

Location: 6 miles west of Reading. 12 miles east of Newbury.
1 1/2 miles from exit 12 of M4 at Theale.
Entrance gate on A340 Road to Pangbourne (3 miles).

Please quote this guide when booking

Savill Garden - Windsor Great Park   Berkshire

World renowned 35 acre woodland garden within Windsor Great Park which was created in 1932 by Sir Eric Savill from an undeveloped area of the Park. Spectacular Spring displays: formal rose gardens and herbaceous borders in Summer; fiery colours of Autumn and misty vistas of Winter. The unique temperate house shelters frost-tender plants from the rigours of Winter - 'a piece of woodland under glass".

Our exciting new visitor centre will open at Easter 2006. This unique building will offer excellent visitor facilities, shop, planteria and restaurant.

The building is an attraction in itself, having a gridshell roof which, together with the floor, is made from timber harvested from the Windsor Estate.

This is the first stage of the restoration of The Royal Landscape project which will evolve over the next few years.

Fact File

Opening Times:	10am - 6pm March - October, 10am - 4pm November - February.
Admission Rates:	Seasonal - Adults £4.00 - £5.50, Senior Citizen £3.60 - £4.95, Child £2.00 - £2.75
Group Rates:	Minimum group size: 10
	Seasonal - Adults £3.20 - £4.40.
Facilities:	Shop, Plant Sales, Teas, Restaurant.
Disabled Access:	Yes. Toilet and Parking for disabled on site. Wheelchairs on loan.
Tours/Events:	Guided tours for groups, bookable in advance.
	On-going programme of events - please contact for details.
Coach Parking:	Yes.
Length of Visit:	3 - 4 hours
Booking Contact:	Julie Hill
	Crown Estate Office, The Great Park, Windsor, Berkshire, SL4 2HT
	Telephone: 01753 847518 Fax: 01753 847536
Email:	savillgarden@thecrownestate.co.uk
Website:	www.savillgarden.co.uk
Location:	Clearly signposted from Ascot, Bagshot, Egham, Windsor, Old Windsor and A30.

Valley Gardens - Windsor Great Park   Surrey

A woodland garden on the grand scale; set beneath the canopies of beautiful mature trees with delightful views to Virginia Water Lake. Over 200 acres of camellias rhododendrons, magnolias and many other flowering trees and shrubs provide visitors with breathtaking displays in March, April and May.

Massed plantings of hydrangeas are the highlight of the summer before a myriad of autumn tints from Japanese maples, birches, sweet gums and tupelos light up the woods.

Winter brings the flowers of witch-hazel and drifts of heathers amongst the dwarf conifers in the Heather Garden before swathes of dwarf daffodils stud the turf in the sweeping Azalea Valley.

Truly a garden for all seasons.

Fact File

Opening Times:	Car park open: 8am - 7pm (4pm in winter) or sunset if earlier.
Admission Rates:	(2005) Car Park Charges only: April & May £5.50, June - March £4.00
Facilities:	At nearby Savill Garden.
Disabled Access:	Yes, but limited. Toilet and parking for disabled on site.
Tours/Events:	None.
Coach Parking:	Coaches by arrangement on weekdays only (Charge applies).
Length of Visit:	2 - 3 hours
Booking Contact:	Julie Hill
	Valley Gardens - The Great Park, Windsor, Berkshire, SL4 2HT
	Telephone: 01753 847518 Fax: 01753 847536
Email:	savillgarden@thecrownestate.co.uk
Website:	www.theroyallandscape.co.uk
Location:	On the eastern boundary of Windsor Great Park (off A30)
	Access to Valley Gardens car park via Wick Road.

Please quote this guide when booking

With a history dating back for a thousand years, Waltham Place has entered a new era. Within the formal layout of mellow brick walls, some dating back to the 17th Century, lie ornamental gardens planted in the new naturalistic style created by Henk Gerritsen where weeds meet garden plants in an ancient framework of wonderful specimen trees.

With organic kitchen garden and farm, several walled gardens, grasspath maze, lake and woodland with Bluebells, Camellias and Rhododendrons.

Explore the boundries between nature and garden in our 170 acre nature inspired paradise.

Fact File

Opening Times:	May to September; Wednesday & Fridays 10am - 4pm (Wednesday for NGS, Fridays by appointment only). Tea Room and Farmshop open Tuesday to Friday
Admission Rates:	Adults £3.50, Senior Citizen £3.50, Child £1.00
Facilities:	Organic Farm Shop, Tea Room, Plant Sales, Education Visits.
Disabled Access:	Yes. Toilet and parking for disabled on site.
Tours/Events:	Seasonal walks, group tours by arrangement.
Coach Parking:	not on site but very close by.
Length of Visit:	2 hours
Booking Contact:	Estate Office Waltham Place, Church Hill, White Waltham, Berks SL6 3JH Telephone: 01628 825517 Fax: 01628 825045
Email:	estateoffice@walthamplace.com
Website:	www.walthamplace.com
Location:	From M4 junction 8/9 take A404M and follow signs to White Waltham. Turn left to Windsor and Paley Street. Farm on left handside.

Please quote this guide when booking

Waddesdon Manor and Gardens were bequeathed to the National Trust by the Rothschilds in 1957. The Gardens today are essentially the ones laid out by Baron Ferdinand de Rothschild and his French landscape designer, Elie Lainé in the 19th century. They are one of the finest Victorian gardens in Britain, and can be enjoyed at any season with a parterre, seasonal displays, rose garden, fountains, statuary, walks and views. At the heart of the Gardens is the Aviary stocked with exotic birds and known for breeding endangered species.

Top quality food and wines are served throughout the day in the restaurants, and the shops offer a superb range of gifts and wines, many of which are unique to Waddesdon.

Conveniently located Waddesdon Manor offers a memorable day out.

Fact File

Opening Times:	Gardens - Weekends in Jan, Feb & Mar (from Jan 7th). 29th March - 23rd December (Wed to Sun, including Mon 18th and Tues 19th December) 10am - 5pm.
Admission Rates:	Adults £5.00, Child £2.50, National Trust Members free. Family £12.50.
Group Rates:	Minimum group size: 15 (Weekdays only) Adults £4.00, Child £2.00, National Trust Members free.
Facilities:	Gift & Wine Shops, Manor & Stables Restaurants.
Disabled Access:	Yes. Toilet and parking for disabled on site. Wheelchairs on loan.
Tours/Events:	Contact the booking office for details.
Coach Parking:	Yes.
Length of Visit:	Minimum 2 hours.
Booking Contact:	Deborah Read. Waddesdon, Nr Aylesbury, Buckinghamshire, HP18 0JH Tel: 01296 653226 Fax: 01296 653212
Email:	deborah.read@nationaltrust.org.uk
Website:	www.waddesdon.org.uk
Location:	On the A41 between Aylesbury & Bicester.

Please quote this guide when booking

A beautiful 4-acre garden, situated behind Elgood's Brewery, on the banks of the River Nene in Wisbech, in the heart of the Fens.

The garden is famous for its maze and its trees, some over 200 years old, including Ginkgo Biloba, Tulip Tree, and Tree of Heaven. There is a lake with golden and ghost carp, a pond, which is home to Great Crested Newts, and a hot-house with many exotic plants.

The Visitor Centre houses a museum with brewery artefacts and pub memorabilia. A variety of freshly prepared snacks are available in the licensed cafe-bar and there is a well-stocked shop selling quality beers, gifts and plants.

Close by are The Octavia Hill Museum, The Wisbech & Fenland Museum, and the National Trust's Peckover House. These attractions, together with several excellent pubs along the riverbanks, add up to an interesting and unusual visit.

Fact File

Opening Times:	2nd May - 28th September 2006 11.30am - 4.30pm.
Admission Rates:	Garden & Brewery - Adults £6.00, Senior Citizens £6.00, Child (6-16) £4.00
	Garden only - Adults £2.50, Senior Citizen £2.00, Child £2.00
Groups Rates:	Minimum group size Daytime 10, Evening 20
	Garden & Brewery - £5.00, Garden Only - £2.00
Facilities:	Visitor Centre, Gift Shop, Plant Sales, Teas, Licensed bar, Free Parking.
	No dogs except guide dogs.
Disabled Access:	Yes. Toilets and parking for disabled on site. Wheelchairs on loan. Booking Advisable.
Tours/Events:	Brewery Tours Tues, Wed, and Thurs 2pm (not suitable for disabled)
Coach Parking:	Yes
Length of Visit:	1 - 2+ Hours
Booking Contact:	Kate Pateman
	North Brink, Wisbech, Cambridge, PE13 1LN
	Telephone: 01945 583160 Fax: 01945 587711
Email:	info@elgoods-brewery.co.uk
Website:	www.elgoods-brewery.co.uk
Location:	Wisbech

Please quote this guide when booking

A Storybook garden for children of any age - but there is much more than a garden here, for the wonderful moated Norman Manor, c.1130, is one of the three oldest continuously inhabited houses in England. It was the home of Lucy Boston from 1939 and the setting for her Green Knowe children's books. She started the garden by planting yew bushes and for the Queen's Coronation cut them into crowns and orbs, later creating chess pieces which now stand in black and white squares. She filled long parallel borders with old-fashioned roses and scented perennials. To begin with, Graham Stuart Thomas advised Lucy on the choice of roses and bearded irises (many of the latter are Dykes Medal winners). At the Norman front are ancient yews and a superb copper beech that has layered itself. Parts of the garden are left wild deliberately.

Fact File

Opening Times: Daily, All Year, 11am - 5pm (4pm in Winter) House is also open but by appointment only.

Admission Rates: Adults £2.00, Senior Citizen £2.00, Child Free.

Facilities: Gift Shop, Plant Sales.

Disabled Access: Partial. Toilet (for emergency use only) and parking (2 cars at house only) for disabled on site.

Tours/Events: None

Coach Parking: No, but nearby

Length of Visit: 1 + hours

Booking Contact: Mrs Diana Boston
The Manor, Hemingford Grey, Huntingdon, Cambridgeshire, PE28 9BN
Telephone: 01480 463134 Fax: 01480 465026

Email: diana_boston@hotmail.com

Website: www.greenknowe.co.uk

Location: By Car - Hemingford Grey is 4 miles south-east of Huntingdon, just off the A14.
By Train - To Huntingdon on Kings Cross line and then Bus or Taxi.
By Bus - No 5 Cambridge - Huntingdon, Bus stops in Hemingford Grey.

Please quote this guide when booking

Set in the heart of the Cheshire countryside, Adlington Hall has been the home of the Legh family since 1315. The Hall itself, a magnificent English country house, incorporates Tudor, Elizabethan and Georgian architecture and houses a 17th century organ played by Handel.

The 2,000 acre Estate, landscaped in the 18th century, contains beautiful gardens in the style of 'Capability' Brown complete with a ha-ha. The ancient Lime Avenue, dating from 1688, leads to a woodland 'Wilderness' with winding paths, temples, bridges and follies. A path through the Laburnum Arcade leads into the formal Rose Garden, then on to the Maze created in English Yew. The Father Tiber Water Garden provides a peaceful haven with its ponds, fountains and water cascade and the newly created parterre provides a colourful addition to the East Wing. Other features include a large herbaceous border, rockeries, specimen trees, azaleas and rhododendrons.

Fact File

Opening Times:	June, July, August: Wednesday only 2pm - 5pm.
	Open weekdays throughout the year for groups by prior arrangement.
Admission Rates:	House and Gardens: Adults £6.00, Senior Citizens £5.00, Child £3.00.
	Gardens only: Adults £2.00, Child £1.00.
Groups Rates:	Minimum group size: 20
	Adults £5.50, Senior Citizens £4.00, Child £2.00.
Facilities:	Tea Room.
Disabled Access:	Limited. Toilet and parking for disabled on site.
Tours/Events:	Guided tours by appointment. Please telephone for details of special events.
Coach Parking:	Yes
Length of Visit:	3 hours
Booking Contact:	The Guide
	Adlington Hall, Adlington. Macclesfield, Cheshire, SK10 4LF
	Telephone: 01625 820875 Fax: 01625 828756
Email:	enquiries@adlingtonhall.com
Website:	www. adlingtonhall.com
Location:	5 miles north of Macclesfield off A523 turn left at Adlington crossroads onto Mill Lane. Entrance 1/2 mile on left.

Please quote this guide when booking

Arley Hall & Gardens — Cheshire

These delightful Grade II* listed gardens have been lovingly created by generations of the same family for over 500 years and the tradition continues today with Viscount Ashbrook. Over the past 30 years he has improved the Grove and Woodland Walk, a less formal area of the garden, planting over 200 rhododendrons, azaleas, exotic trees and shrubs.

Paths lead you in and out of smaller gardens, each with a different theme and character, from the shaded herb garden to the flag garden and on to "the oldest and finest double herbaceous border in the country". From icy whites, silvers and pale blues in April and May to fiery reds, opulent oranges and deep golds in September, the borders continue to enthral visitors.

Events include outdoor concerts, antique and craft fairs, the Arley Horse Trials & Country Fair, Arley Garden Festival and Spring Plant Fair.

Fact File

Opening Times: 1 April – 2 October 2006: Tuesday – Sunday: 11 a.m. – 5 p.m. Closed Monday (Hall open Tuesday and Sunday only)

Admission Rates: Adults: (Gardens) £5.00, Senior Citizens: £4.50, Children: £2.00

Group Rates: Minimum Groups Size: 15 Adults (Gardens): £4.50, Senior Citizens: £4.00

Facilities: Shop, Plant Sales, Licensed Restaurant, Teas, Picnic Area, Play Area, Chapel, Estate Walks.

Disabled Access: Yes. Toilet and parking on site. Wheelchair Loan booking available (recommended for special events).

Tours/Events: Guided tours available. Spring Plant Fair – 2 April, 24 – 25 June: Arley Garden Festival.

Coach Parking: Yes.

Length of Visit: 2 hours

Booking Contact Caroline Fearon
Arley Hall & Gardens, Northwich, Cheshire CW9 6NA
Telephone: 01565 777353 Fax: 01565 777465

Email: caroline.fearon@arleyhallandgardens.com

Website: www.arleyhallandgardens.com

Location: M6 – Junction 19 or 20, M56 Junction 10. Brown tourist signs from Northwich and Knutsford, both 6 miles approximately.

Please quote this guide when booking

Cholmondeley Castle Garden

Cholmondeley Castle Garden is said by many to be among the most romantically beautiful gardens they have seen. Even the wild orchids, daisies and buttercups take on an aura of glamour in this beautifully landscaped setting. Visitors enter by the deer park mere - one of two strips of water which are home to many types of waterfowl and freshwater fish. Those who take advantage of the picnic site can walk round the lake and enjoy the splendid view of the Gothic Castle which stands so dramitically on the hill surrounded by sweeping lawns and magnificent trees; two enormous cedars of lebanon and great spreading oaks among sweet chestnut, lime, beech and plane. Whatever the season there is always a wealth of plants and shrubs in flower from the earliest bulbs through many varieties of magnolia, camellia, azalea and rhododendrons. Followed by a golden canopied laburnum grove, a very fine davidia involucrata in the glade, and varieties of cornus. There is also a very pretty rose garden surrounded by mixed borders, containing a large variety of herbaceous plants and shrubs.

Fact File

Opening Times:	April to September. (Castle not open to public). Wednesday, Thursday, Sunday (Bank Holidays and Good Friday).
Admission Rates:	Adults £4.00, Child £1.50.
Group Rates:	Minimum group size: 25
Facilities:	Shop, Plant Sales, Teas.
Disabled Access:	Yes. Toilet and parking for disabled on site,
Tours/Events:	Please ring to enquire about special events, plant fares, plays, concerts.
Coach Parking:	Yes
Length of Visit:	3 - 4 hours
Booking Contact:	Cholmondeley Castle, Malpas, Cheshire, SY14 8AH Telephone: 01829 720383 Fax: 01829 720877
Email:	penny@cholmondeleycastle.co.uk
Website:	None.
Location:	7 miles west of Nantwich, 6 miles north of Whitchurch on A49.

Please quote this guide when booking

Rode Hall Gardens

Rode Hall Gardens were created by three notable landscape designers; Humphry Repton drew up the plans for the landscape and Rode Pool in his 'Red Book' of 1790. Between 1800 and 1810 John Webb, a Cheshire landscapist, constructed the Pool, an artificial lake of approximately 40 acres and at the same time he created the terraced rock garden and grotto. This area is covered in snowdrops in February followed by daffodils and bluebells and colour continues with the flowering of many specie and hybrid rhododendrons and azaleas in May.

In 1860 William Nesfield designed the rose garden and terrace where the flowerbeds are now filled with roses and a variety of herbaceous plants.

The two-acre walled kitchen garden dates from 1750 and grows a wide variety of flowers, vegetables and fruit.

There is a fine icehouse and the Hall is open to the public on Wednesdays.

Fact File

Opening Times:	Snowdrop walks: Saturday 4 February to Sunday 26 February –daily except Mondays: 12–4pm. 1 April to 30 September: Tuesdays, Wednesdays, Thursdays and Bank Holidays (not Good Friday): 2 – 5pm.
Admission Rates:	Adults: £3.00, Senior Citizens £2.50, Children (over 12): £2.50
Group Rates:	Minimum Groups Size: 15
Facilities:	Shop, plant sales, teas, light lunches for snowdrop walkers in February only.
Disabled Access:	Limited. Toilet and car parking on site
Tours/Events:	Guided tours available.
Coach Parking:	Yes
Length of Visit:	1 hour.
Booking Contact:	Valerie Stretton. Rode Hall Gardens, Rode Hall, Scholar Green, Cheshire ST7 3QN Telephone: 01270 882961 Fax: 01270 882962
Email:	rodehall@scholargreen.fsnet.co.uk
Website:	www.rodehall.co.uk
Location:	5 miles south of Congleton, between A34 and A50.

Please quote this guide when booking

Stapeley Water Gardens   Cheshire

Visit this all year round attraction for a fantastic day out! The Garden Centre provides a great shopping experience, with fabulous selection of plants, gifts, pets, fish, water gardening and much more! Relax by the display gardens and gain inspiration from the pools and marvel at the National Collection of Water Lilies, in bloom from mid June to mid September.

The Palms Tropical Oasis offers a truly unique experience, with an extensive zoological collection, including Baby Black Tipped Reef Sharks, Cotton Top Tamarin Monkeys, Toco Toucans and much more! This tropical paradise, with its cascading waters and exotic fish and plants – including Giant Amazon Water Lily – provides a stunning environment. You can also take a stroll in the beautiful Italian Gardens. Enjoy a snack in their café, or a full meal in the Restaurant with a varied and delicious menu.

Fact File

Opening Times:	Garden Centre: 9am–6pm. (summer), 9am – 5pm. (winter), Sundays: 10am– 4pm.
	Palms, Tropical Oasis: 10am–6pm. (summer), 10am– 5pm. (winter), Sundays: 10am– 5pm.
Admission Rates:	(Admission to Palms Tropical Oasis only)
	Adults: £4.45, Senior Citizens: £3.95, Children: £2.60
Group Rates:	Minimum Groups Size: 15
Facilities:	Shop, plant sales, restaurant, teas. Feeding schedule at the Palms Tropical Oasis every Sunday, plus a choice of three group entertainment packages (please request a leaflet).
Disabled Access:	Yes. Toilet and car parking on site. Wheelchair Loan booking available.
Tours/Events:	Guided tours available with meal package.
Coach Parking:	Yes
Length of Visit:	Approximately 3 hours.
Booking Contact	Palms Reception. Stapeley Water Gardens, London Road, Nantwich, Cheshire. CW5 7LH
	Telephone: 01270 628628 Fax: 01270 624188
Email:	palms@stapeleywg.com
Website:	www.stapeleywg.com
Location:	Signposted from J16, M6. 1 mile south of Nantwich on A51

Please quote this guide when booking

(Photograph by Val Anderson)

Approximately 100 acres of Woodland Gardens and natural woodland bordering the Lynher Estuary featuring extensive woodlands and riverside walks.

The garden contains the national collection of *Camellia japonica*. There are a wide variety of camellias, magnolias, rhododendrons and other flowering trees and shrubs, numerous wild flowers and birds in beautiful surrounds.

Fact File

Opening Times: 11am to 5.30pm, everyday excluding Mondays and Fridays. Open Bank holiday Mondays and Good Friday. 1st March to 31st October.

Admission Rates: Adults £4.00, Senior Citizen £4.00, Child under 16 free.

Group Rates: As admission rates.

Facilities: Teas, Restaurant, shop (Available on Antony House open days).

Disabled Access: Yes over rough terrain in parts. Parking for disabled on site.

Tours/Events: Tours available for parties on request.

Coach Parking: Yes

Length of Visit: between 1 - 2 hours

Booking Contact: Mrs V Anderson
Antony, Torpoint, Cornwall, PL11 2QA
Telephone: 01752 812364

Email: pcressy@savills.com

Website: None

Location: From the A38 Trerulefoot roundabout follow brown tourist signs for Antony House.
At Antony House continue past the house down the drive. The Woodland Gardens can be found on the left hand side.

Please quote this guide when booking

Boconnoc, an important house for 1000 years, will host the vibrant 2006 Cornwall Spring Flower Show; but the layers of its history reach back to the ancient deer park graced by veteran trees clothed by rare ferns and mosses.

The picturesque park holds the echoes of many generations. The Obelisk at 123 feet is the largest, the Clump planted to commemorate the death of the Duke of Wellington the most evocative and the leat which feeds water through the gardens the most fascinating. The elegant Bathhouse speaks of the early 19th Century while the long drives and Pinetum created by G.M. Fortescue tell of the golden years after 1840.

Rhododendrons, azaleas and hydrangeas are companions to the rarer trees and shrubs in the Dorothy Garden, the Shrubbery and the Stewardry Walk; all made popular by openings under the National Gardens Scheme.

The Boconnoc House restoration project is open for group visits. Coach parties are welcome.

Fact File

Opening Times:	Group visits by appointment at any time to House and Garden. Gardens open Sunday April 23, 30, May 7, 14, 21, 28.
Admission Rates:	Gardens: Adults: £4.50, Children: Under 12 free. House: £3.00
Group Rates:	Minimum Groups Size: 15
Facilities:	Talks given before guided tours. Lunches in stableyard or dining room, by arrangement.
Disabled Access:	Yes. Car parking and W.C on site.
Tours/Events:	Guided tours available. Cornwall Spring Flower Show 1st, 2nd April. House and Garden Fair 16th, 17th May Boconnoc Steam Fair 21st – 23rd July Open-air theatre 30th July and 23rd August
Coach Parking:	Yes
Length of Visit:	1½ hours – 5 hours.
Booking Contact	Mrs. Knapman Boconnoc, The Estate Office, Boconnoc, Lostwithiel, Cornwall PL22 0RG. Telephone: 01208 872507 Fax: 01208 873836
Email:	adgfortescue@btinternet.com **Website:** www.boconnocenterprises.co.uk
Location:	SX 147607 on A390. Enter by Middle Taphouse, follow signs (Boconnoc is between Liskeard and Fowey).

Please quote this guide when booking

Caerhays Castle Gardens   Cornwall

Magnificent Magnolias, robust Rhododendrons, championship Camellias, colours which range from pure white to deepest purple, everywhere you look a vista of exciting sizes, shapes, colours and smells assault your senses in this outstanding spring woodland garden. Acers, Oaks and native woodland trees are complemented by swathes of pale primroses, brilliant golden daffodils, sparkling bluebells.

Holders of a NCCPG National Magnolia Collection and home to the world famous x williamsii Camellias, Caerhays Castle Gardens still have some original plants collected for them by the intrepid plant collectors in the early 1900s, these grow happily alongside modern hybrids bred by the Williams family, owners for over 150 years.

With several different routes around the gardens both experienced and amateur gardeners or anyone with a love of nature will find something of interest in this 60 acres of heaven situated in a sheltered valley overlooking Porthluny Beach.

Fact File

Opening Times: Garden: 13.2.2006 – 31.5.2006: 10 a.m. – 5 p.m. – last entry 4 p.m.
House: 13.3.2006 – 31.5.2006: weekdays only, 12noon – 4 p.m

Admission Rates: Adults: £5.50, Senior Citizens: £5.00, Children: £2.50.

Group Rates: Minimum Groups Size: 15
Adults/Senior Citizens: From £4.00, Children: From £2.00.

Facilities: Shop, plant sales, restaurant/tea rooms.

Disabled Access: Yes- part. Toilet and car parking on site.

Tours/Events: Guided tours available.

Coach Parking: Yes.

Length of Visit: Garden: 2 – 2$1/2$ hours. House: 1 hour.

Booking Contact Cheryl Kufel
Caerhays Castle Gardens, Estate Office, Caerhays, Gorran, St. Austell, Cornwall PL26 6LY
Telephone: 01872 501310 Fax: 01872 501870

Email: estateoffice@caerhays.co.uk

Website: www.caerhays.co.uk

Location: Turn right of A390 near Grampound and follow signs to Caerhays.
Parking at beach at bottom of hill.

Please quote this guide when booking

Lush, unmanicured and utterly magical, Carwinion Garden lies in a sheltered Cornish valley on the Helford River. Ponds, waterfalls and sheltered pathways are dotted amongst the towering trees, bamboos and well-established plants in this twelve acre family run garden.

The garden contains a plethora of specimen plants, immense tree ferns over a hundred years old, gunnera with leaves spanning over two metres and ferns and Hellebores which flourish in the dappled sunlit woodland. Carwinion has one of the largest collections of bamboos in England; over a hundred and sixty different varieties can be found growing throughout the garden.

The garden is at its pinnacle in Spring-time when the impact of colour, the bluebell carpeted woodland, the fragrance of the Azaleas and the continued blooming of the Camellias provides a sensual experience not to be missed.

Fact File

Opening Times:	All Year, every day 10am - 5.30pm
Admission Rates:	Adults £3.50, Senior Citizens £3.50, Child Free (under 16).
Group Rates:	Minimum group size: 10
	Adults £3.00, Senior Citizens £3.00.
Facilities:	Plant Sales, Teas (2 - 5.30pm from May - Sept), Small Gift Shop.
Disabled Access:	Partial. Toilet and parking for disabled on site.
Tours/Events:	Occasional Art Exhibits & Theatre displayed in Gardens and House.
Coach Parking:	yes, by arrangement
Length of Visit:	1 - 2 hours
Booking Contact:	Jane Rogers
	Carwinion, Carwinion Road, Mawnan Smith, Nr Falmouth, Cornwall, TR11 5JA
	Telephone: 01326 250258 Fax: 01326 250903
Email:	jane@carwinion.freeserve.co.uk
Website:	www.carwinion.com
Location:	Five miles South-West of Falmouth, in the village of Mawnan Smith, North side of the Helford River.

Please quote this guide when booking

Cotehele Garden   Cornwall

Cotehele, owned by the Edgecumbe family for nearly 600 years, is a fascinating and enchanting estate set on the steep wooded slopes of the River Tamar. Exploring Cotehele's many and various charms provides a full day out for the family and leaves everyone longing to return.

A walk through the garden and along the river leads to the quay where the restored Tamar sailing barge *shamrock* is moored. Cotehele Mill is to be found tucked away in the woods. Restored to working order and now grinding corn to produce flour, (which can be purchased) the 0.3mile walk from the Quay is a must.

Fact File

Opening Times:	House: 18th March - 31st October. Garden: all year round 10.30 - dusk.
Admission Rates:	Adults £4.80, Child £2.40.
Group Rates:	Minimum group size: 15 +
Facilities:	Shop, Plant Sales, Gallery, Teas and Restaurant.
Disabled Access:	Partial. Toilet and parking for disabled on site. Wheelchairs on loan.
Tours/Events:	Garden Tours available upon request for groups £3.00 pp.
Coach Parking:	Yes
Length of Visit:	3 hours
Booking Contact:	Leesa Clements
	Cotehele, St Dominic, Saltash, Cornwall. PL12 6TA
	Telephone: 01579 351346 Fax: 01579 351222
Email:	cotehele@nationaltrust.org.uk
Website:	www.nationaltrust.org.uk
Location:	On the west (Cornish) bank of the Tamar, 8 miles SW of Tavistock, 14 miles east of St Dominick.

Please quote this guide when booking

The Lost Gardens of Heligan   Cornwall

Heligan, seat of the Tremayne family for more than 400 years, is one of the most mysterious estates in England. At the end of the nineteenth century its thousand acres were at their zenith; but only a few years after the Great War of 1914, bramble and ivy were already drawing a green veil over this sleeping beauty.

After decades of neglect, the devastating hurricane of 1990 should have consigned the Lost Gardens of Heligan to a footnote in history. Instead, fired by a magnificent obsession to bring these once glorious gardens back to life, a small band of enthusiasts has grown into a large working team with its own vision for Heligan's future.

Today "The Nation's Favourite Garden" offers 200 acres for exploration including restored productive gardens, working buildings and historic glasshouses, atmospheric pleasure grounds and a subtropical "Jungle" valley, surrounded by a sustainably managed estate incorporating a pioneering wildlife conservation project.

Fact File

Opening Times: From 10am daily, all year round.

Admission Rates: Adults £7.50, Senior Citizens £7.00, Child £4.00, Family (2 adults and 3 children) £20.00

Groups Rates: Minimum group size 20, prior booking is essential.
Adults £7.00, Senior Citizens £6.50, Child £4.00. Pre-booked guided tour additional £1pp.

Facilities: Licensed Tea Rooms, Lunchtime Servery, Heligan Shop and Plant Sales, Lobbs Farm Shop. No Dogs March - October incl.

Disabled Access: Yes. All facilities and throughout most of the garden restoration and wildlife hide. Wheelchairs are available on a first come first served basis. Contact us for information in various formats.

Tours/Events: Please telephone for seasonal details or see our website.

Coach Parking: Yes, by prior arrangement.

Length of Visit: At least 4 hours

Booking Contact: Group Bookings Department.
The Lost Gardens of Heligan, Pentewan, St Austell, Cornwall, PL26 6EN.
Telephone: 01726 845120   Fax: 01726 845101

Email: info@heligan.com

Website: www.heligan.com

Location: From St Austell, take the Mevagissey Road (B3273) and follow the brown tourist signs to "The Lost Gardens of Heligan".

Please quote this guide when booking

One of only three Grade 1 listed Cornish Gardens set within the 865 acres of the Country Park overlooking Plymouth Sound. Sir Richard Edgcumbe of Cotehele built a new home in his deer park at Mount Edgcumbe in 1547. Miraculously the walls of this red stone Tudor House survived a direct hit by bombs in 1941 and it was restored by the 6th Earl in 1958. It is now beautifully furnished with family possessions.

The two acre Earl's Garden was created beside the House in the 18th century. Ancient and rare trees including a 400 year old lime, a splendid Lucombe oak and a Mexican pine, are set amidst classical garden houses and an exotic Shell Seat. Colourful flowers and heather grace the re-created Victorian East Lawn terrace. Also formal 18th Century Gardens in Italian, French & English style, modern American & New Zealand sections. There are over 1000 varieties in the National Camellia Collection which received the international award of 'Camellia Garden of Excellence'.

Fact File

Opening Times: House & Earls Garden open 2nd April - 28th September, Sunday to Thursday
11am - 4.30pm; Country Park open all year.

Admission Rates: Adults £4.50, Senior Citizen £3.50, Child £2.25

Groups Rates: Minimum group size: 10 (March - October)
Adults £3.50, Senior Citizen £3.50, Child £2.00

Facilities: Shop & Tea Room in House.
Orangery Restaurant (limited opening in winter), Civil Weddings, Conference Facilities.

Disabled Access: Yes. Toilet and parking for disabled on site. Wheelchairs on loan, booking necessary.

Tours/Events: Guided tours of the gardens available all year. Historic buildings, Camellia Collection in season. Exhibition and events programme. Introductory talk given to booked groups.

Coach Parking: Yes

Length of Visit: 2 hours

Booking Contact: Secretary. Mount Edgcumbe House, Cremyll, Torpoint, Cornwall, PL10 1HZ
Telephone : 01752 822236 Fax: 01752 822199

Email: mt.edgcumbe@plymouth.gov.uk

Website: www.mountedgcumbe.gov.uk

Location: FromPlymouth Cremyll Foot Ferry, Torpoint Ferry or Saltash Bridge.
From Cornwall via Liskeard - to A374, B3247, follow brown signs.

Please quote this guide when booking

Pencarrow, a Georgian house with 50 acres of Grade 2* listed Gardens, must be one of Cornwall's finest stately homes. It is still privately owned and lived in by the Molesworth-St Aubyn's, who purchased the estate in the reign of Queen Elizabeth I. Pencarrow lies at the foot of a valley midway between Bodmin and Wadebridge. It is approached through a mile long drive flanked by well planned woodland, nearly 700 varieties of rhododendrons, camellias and hydrangeas.

The imposing Palladian style house built in 1771, contains a superb collection of paintings by many famous artists, including a unique collection of works by Sir Joshua Reynolds, set amongst outstanding furniture and porcelain. In 1882 during his visit Sir Arthur Sullivan composed much of the music for his comic opera 'Iolanthe". Pencarrow was NPI National Heritage Award winner (also voted by its visitors "Best Historic House in the United Kingdom"). In 2004 it received The Dogs' Trust national award as Dogs' Tourist attraction of the year.

Fact File

Opening Times:	The house is open Sun to Thurs 2nd April to 26th October, 11am-5pm (last tour 4pm). The Gardens are open 7 days a week 1st March to 31st October 9.30am - 5.30pm.
Admission Rates:	House & Gardens: Adults £8.00, Child £4.00. Gardens only: Adults £4.00, Child £1.00
Groups Rates:	Minimum group size: 20 - 30, Adults £7.00, Child £3.50 31 + Adults £6.00, Child £3.00
Facilities:	House, Shop, Craft Gallery, Plant Sales, Children's Play Area, Tea Rooms serving light lunches and cream teas.
Disabled Access:	Yes. Toilet and parking for disabled on site.
Tours/Events:	Guided tours around the house (last tour 4pm) - Garden tours for group bookings. Jazz in Gardens, Theatre, Concerts, Conference Room, Wedding License.
Coach Parking:	Yes.
Length of Visit:	2 1/2 - 5 hours
Booking Contact:	James Reynolds. Pencarrow, Washaway, Bodmin, Cornwall, PL30 3AG. Telephone: 01208 841369 Fax: 01208 841722
Email:	info@pencarrow.co.uk
Website:	www.pencarrow.co.uk
Location:	Four miles north west of Bodmin, signed off the A389 and B3266 at Washaway.

Please quote this guide when booking

Penjerrick Garden   Cornwall

'Few gardens have the wonderful atmosphere of Penjerrick, another creation of the Fox family, the great Cornish master gardeners. Penjerrick has a valley site sloping towards the sea. But here there is a character of wildness which provides exactly the right contrast to some of the more swaggering rhododendrons which are such a striking feature of the garden. Superlative old beeches, copper and ordinary, date from the early 1800s and provide a stately background to more exotic planting.' (Quotation – Patrick Taylor).

Penjerrick is a 15 acre Grade II listed Spring flowering garden containing rhododendrons, camellias, bamboos, magnolias, azaleas and some magnificent trees.

The lower valley garden, reached by a wooden bridge, contains a network of ponds, giant tree ferns and gunnera in a wild, somewhat primeval woodland setting. It preserves a jungle-like exuberance and visitors, if suitably booted, should enjoy their experience.

Fact File

Opening Times:	Wednesdays, Fridays and Sundays March – end September, 1.30am – 4.30pm Coach parties welcome any day, mornings preferred, but prior booking please.
Admission Rates:	Adults: £2.50, Senior Citizens: £2.50, Children: £1.00
Group Rates:	Minimum Groups Size: Any (no group rates).
Facilities:	None, but Penmorvah Hotel opposite entrance has.
Disabled Access:	No.
Tours/Events:	No.
Coach Parking:	Yes, one coach at gate 200 yards from garden. (Car parking on site).
Length of Visit:	1- 2 hours
Booking Contact:	Rachel Morin
	Penjerrick Garden, Budock Water, Nr. Falmouth, Cornwall, TR11 5ED
	Telephone: 01872 870105
Website:	www.penjerrickgarden.co.uk
Location:	Three miles south-west of Falmouth, between villages of Budock and Mawnan Smith.
	Coach access via Budock (not Mabe/Argal as lanes too narrow)

Please quote this guide when booking

Pine Lodge Gardens & Nursery   Cornwall

The 30- acre estate comprises gardens within a garden which hold a wide range of some 6000 plants, all of which are labelled. In addition to rhododendrons, magnolias and camellias so familiar in Cornish gardens here are Mediterranean and southern-hemisphere plants grown for all year round interest. Herbaceous borders, a fernery, a formal garden, a woodland walk, shrubberies and a wild flower meadow.

The water features include a large wildlife pond, an ornamental pond with cascades (stocked with koi carp), a lake with an island (home for black swans and water fowl) and marsh gardens. Trees are also a speciality with an acer glade, a collection of 80 conifers, all different, in a four acre Pinetum, an Arboretum and an acre Japanese garden. Holder of the National collection of Grevilleas. Seeds brough back on Seed Hunting Exhibitions every year for our Nursery of Rare & Unusual Plants. The gardens were given a Highly Commended Award by the Cornish Tourist Board for 2002.

Fact File

Opening Times:	All year except 24th, 25th & 26th December. Nursery open all year.
Admission Rates:	Adults £5.50, Child £3.00.
Groups Rates:	Minimum group size: 20 - Adults £5.00
Facilities:	Plant Sales, Tea Room, Shop.
Disabled Access:	Partial. Toilet and parking for disabled on site, Wheelchairs on loan, booking necessary.
Tours/Events:	Tours everyday, booking essential. Wood Turning demonstration everyday.
Coach Parking:	Yes.
Length of Visit:	3 hours
Booking Contact:	Shirley Clemo Pine Lodge Gardens, Holmbush, St Austell, Cornwall, PL25 3RQ Telephone: 01726 73500 Fax: 01726 77370
Email:	garden@pine-lodge.co.uk
Website:	www.pine-lodge.co.uk
Location:	Situated on the A390 2 miles east of St Austell

Please quote this guide when booking

Trebah Garden   Cornwall

Steeply wooded 25 acre sub-tropical ravine garden falls 200 feet from 18th century house to private beach on Helford River.

A Stream cascades over waterfalls through ponds full of Koi Carp and exotic water plants, winds through 2 acres of blue and white hydrangeas and spills out over the beach. Huge Australian tree ferns and palms mingle with shrubs of ever changing colours and scent beneath over-arching canopy of 100 year old rhododendrons and magnolias. A giant plantation of gunnera and clumps of huge bamboos give the garden a unique and exotic wildness matched by no other garden in the British Isles.

The newly built Hibbert Centre houses a distinctive restaurant, garden and gift shop. Children love Trebah, as do dogs (welcome on leads).

Fact File

Opening Times: Open every day of the year 10.30am to 5pm.
Admission Rates: Adults £5.80, Senior Citizen £5.30, Child £2.00. 1st Nov - 28th March, Adults £3.00,
                       Senior Citizen £2.50, Child £1.00. RHS and NT Members Free Nov, Dec, Jan & Feb.
Group Rates: Minimum group size: 12
                       Adults £4.80, Senior Citizen £4.80, Child £2.00.
Facilities: Visitor Centre, Shop, Plant Sales, Teas, Restaurant.
Disabled Access: Yes, Toilet and parking for disabled on site. Wheelchairs on loan, booking advised.
Tours/Events: Free welcome talk on arrival, full guided tour of one and a half hours at an extra
                       £1 per head - must be booked in advance.
Coach Parking: Yes.
Length of Visit: 2 1/2 - 3 hours
Booking Contact: V Woodcroft
                       Trebah Garden, Mawnan Smith, Falmouth, Cornwall, TR11 5JZ.
                       Telephone: 01326 250448 Fax: 01326 250781
Email: mail@trebah-garden.co.uk
Website: www.trebah-garden.co.uk
Location: From north - A39 from Truro to Treliever Cross Roundabout, follow brown and white
                       tourism signs to Trebah.

Please quote this guide when booking

The garden at Tregrehan is a large planted woodland area surrounding a more formal walled garden complete with a fine original glasshouse range. It is listed by English Heritage as outstanding.

A guided tour usually takes two hours, giving time for light refreshments at the conclusion. There is also a small nursery selling plants propagated from the garden. The appeal of visiting Tregrehan lies in the non-commercial approach of the owners and the diversity of the plants grown.

The backbone of the garden is the planting of exotica from the early 19th century onwards, many of which have reached exceptional size for the UK. To compliment this Victorian passion for new plants William Nesfield redesigned in 1845 the more formal areas around the house.

Much planting is still undertaken from known natural sources creating a future Green Gene Bank, within a Temperate Cornish Rainforest!

Fact File

Opening Times:	Mid March - Mid June, Wednesday - Sunday incl. Bank Holiday Mondays (Closed Easter Sunday) 10.30 - 17.00. Also Mid June - End August, Wed 14.00 - 17.00.
Admission Rates:	Adults £4.00, Senior Citizens £4.00, Child Free
Groups Rates:	Minimum group size 10
Facilities:	Plant Sales, Teas
Disabled Access:	Partial (1/2 Garden). Toilet and parking for disabled on site.
Tours/Events:	Guided tours included for groups over 10, by appointment anytime.
Coach Parking:	Yes
Length of Visit:	2 Hours
Booking Contact:	T Hudson Tregrehan House, Par, Cornwall. PL24 2SJ Telephone: 01726 814389 Fax: 01726 814389
Email:	enq@tregrehan.org
Website:	www.tregrehan.org
Location:	On A390 2 miles east of St Austell 1/2 mile west of St Blazey.

Please quote this guide when booking

Where in the world is it possible to bring together garden plants from five different continents and all under the influence of a Mediterranean and maritime climate? The answer of course is Tresco Abbey Garden on the Isles of Scilly. Microclimates within the garden shelterbelts ensure the most unique collection of exotics grown outdoors in the British Isles are available to the enthusiastic garden visitor.

South Africa, California, Australia, Chile, New Zealand, Madeira, Mexico, Brazil and even Burma are just some of the countries represented in this extraordinary and beautiful garden.

Thrown into the middle of the garden one could be forgiven for thinking that they had been transported to the French Riviera with lusty palm trees, hot and colourful succulents and panoramic sea views to rival even the Caribbean. The newly built Garden Visitor Centre with History Room, Shop, Licensed Café and Tea Garden will enhance your day as you reflect upon the splendour of the extravagant plant collection you have just witnessed.

Fact File

Opening Times:	Open every day of the year 10.00 a.m. – 16.00 p.m.
Admission Rates:	Adults: £8.50, Senior Citizens: £8.50, Children: Free under 16
Group Rates:	Minimum Groups Size: 12. Adults: £8.50, Senior Citizens: £8.50, Children: Free under 16
Facilities:	Visitor centre, shop, plant sales, restaurant, teas
Disabled Access:	Yes. Toilet and car parking on site. Wheelchair Loan booking available. Electric buggy available for disabled.
Tours/Events:	Guided tours available.
Coach Parking:	Yes.
Length of Visit:	2 hours.
Booking Contact	Garden Curator, Mike Nelhams
	Tresco Abbey Garden, Tresco, Isles of Scilly, Cornwall TR24 0PQ
	Telephone: 01720 424105
Email:	mikenelhams@tresco.co.uk
Website:	www.tresco.co.uk
Location:	Day trips available by air – B.I.H. Helicpoters direct to Tresco: 01736 363871
	Day trips by sea – Isles of Scilly Steamship Company: 08457 105555.

Please quote this guide when booking

Trevarno Estate & National Museum of Gardening   Cornwall

A unique and unforgettable gardening experience comprising seventy acres of beautiful Victorian and Gardens and Grounds. Trevarno is one of Cornwall's secret jewells having one of the countries largest and most diverse plant collections, abundant wildlife and major restoration projects within the walled gardens. Explore the tranquil woodland walks, including the new 2km Estate Walk, terraces, rockery and grotto, and more formal areas including the Serpentine Yew Tunnel and Italian Garden. Relax in the Fountain Garden Conservatory and enjoy the homemade refreshments. Leave time to visit the unique National Museum of Gardening, Vintage Soap Collection, Toy Museum, Organic Soap and Herbal Workshop and shop. There's also the Woodland Adventure Play Area for the youngsters.

Fact File

Opening Times:	10.30am - 5pm all year except Christmas Day & Boxing Day.
Admission Rates:	Adults £5.15, Senior Citizens £4.45 , Child £1.95, Disabled £2.75.
Group Rates:	Minimum group size: 12
	Adults £4.25, Senior Citizen £3.75, Child £1.25.
Facilities:	The National Museum of Gardening, Shop, Plant Sales, Tea Room, Vintage Soap Collection, Craft Workshops, *Vintage Toy Collection (*small additional charge).
Disabled Access:	Partial. Toilet and parking for disabled on site. Wheelchairs on loan, booking essential.
Tours/Events:	Numerous events throughout the year. Please call for details or visit www.trevarno.co.uk.
Coach Parking:	Yes, for up to 6 coaches.
Length of Visit:	4 hours
Booking Contact:	Garden Co-ordinator
	Trevarno Estate, Trevarno Manor, Crowntown, Nr Helston, Cornwall, TR13 ORU
	Telephone: 01326 574274 Fax: 01326 574282
Email:	enquiry@trevarno.co.uk
Website:	www.trevarno.co.uk
Location:	Trevarno is located immediately east of Crowntown village - leave Helston on Penzance Road and follow the brown signs.

Please quote this guide when booking

Trewithen means 'house of the trees' and the name truly describes this fine early Georgian house in its splendid setting of wood and parkland.

Country Life described the house as 'one of the outstanding West Country houses of the 18th century' and Penelope Hobhouse has described the garden as 'perhaps the most beautiful woodland garden in England'.

2004 was the 100th year in which George Johnstone inherited Trewithen and started developing the gardens as we know them today. The great glade on the south side is a masterpiece of landscape gardening and is a monument to the genius of George Johnstone. These gardens covering some thirty acres are renowned for their magnificent collection of camellias, rhododendrons, magnolias and many rare trees and shrubs which are seldom found elsewhere in Britain. The extensive woodland gardens are surrounded by traditional landscaped parkland.

Fact File

Opening Times:	Open 1st February to 30th September, 10am to 4.30pm Monday to Saturday. Sundays (February to May only).
Admission Rates:	Adults £5.00 Feb to June, £4.50 July to September.
Groups Rate:	Minimum group size: 20 Group £4.50 Feb to June, £4.00 July to September.
Facilities:	Trewithen Tea Shop, Plant Sales, Camera Obscura, Viewing Platforms.
Disabled Access:	Yes. Toilet and Parking for disabled on site. Wheelchairs on loan.
Tours/Events:	Guided tours available, prior booking is essential. Occasional special events please telephone for details.
Coach Parking:	Yes
Length of Visit:	2 - 2 1/2 hours
Booking Contact:	Glenys Cates Trewithen Gardens, Grampound Road, Nr Truro, Cornwall, TR2 4DD Telephone: 01726 883647 Fax: 01726 882301
Email:	gardens@trewithen-estate.demon.co.uk
Website:	www.trewithengardens.co.uk
Location:	On the A390 between Truro and St Austell.

Please quote this guide when booking

Blackwell, The Arts & Crafts House Cumbria

An architectural gem set amidst stunning views of the lake and mountains, Blackwell is one of the most important and rare surviving Arts and Crafts Movement houses in England. Originally built in 1900 as a holiday home, today Blackwell is the only example of the architect M H Baillie Scott's work open to the public. Amazingly, the carved oak panelling, wrought ironwork, Art Nouveau stained glass, intricate plasterwork, stone carving and original fireplaces with William De Morgan tiling have all survived intact.

The gardens were cleverly designed by Thomas Mawson in a series of terraces, bordered by beautiful flower beds with climbing plants and exotic herbs, to make the most of the breathtaking views. This is one of the loveliest places anywhere in England to sit outside and enjoy morning coffee, lunch or afternoon tea overlooking Windermere Lake and Coniston Fells.

Fact File

Opening Times:	13th February - 24th December 2006
Admission Rates:	Adults £5.45 (2006), Discounts for children and families.
Groups Rates:	Minimum group size 10
	Special rates for pre-booked groups and school groups.
Facilities:	Craft and Book Shop, Tearoom, Changing Exhibitions.
Disabled Access:	Partial. Toilets and parking for disabled on site. Wheelchair available for loan. Booking advisable.
Tours/Events:	Please telephone for details.
Coach Parking:	Free coach parking available for pre-booked groups, close to the site.
Length of Visit:	2 hours
Booking Contact:	Catriona Sale
	Blackwell, The Arts & Crafts House, Bowness-On-Windermere, Cumbria LA23 3JR
	Telephone: 015394 46139 Fax: 015394 88486
Email:	info@blackwell.org.uk
Website:	www.blackwell.org.uk
Location:	M6 J36, Blackwell is situated 1 1/2 miles south of Bowness-on-Windermere just off the A5074 on the B5360.

Please quote this guide when booking

Brantwood's gardens and estate are like no other. Mature Victorian landscape gardens lead to Ruskin's own experimental landscapes, to ancient woodlands, high Moorland and spectacular views. Completion of the Zig-Zaggy, a garden begun by John Ruskin 130 years ago, and the High Walk, a spectacular Victorian viewing platform, brings a total of eight gardens restored at Brantwood. Expect the unexpected and explore 250 acres of fascinating landscape.

Whichever season you choose to visit you are assured year round interest. Spectacular azaleas in springtime; a collection of ferns, herbs and colourful herbaceous borders in summer; the vibrant colours of autumn; or a winter snowfall can transform the gardens into a winter wonderland.

Stroll the paths, sit and marvel at the magnificent views. Whatever you choose to do, you will take home with you the discovery of John Ruskin's legacy and inspiration.

Fact File

Opening Times: Mid - March to mid - November daily 11am - 5.30pm.
Mid - November to mid - March Wednesday - Sunday 11am - 4.30pm.
Admission Rates: Adults £5.50 / £3.75 garden only, Child £1.00
Groups Rates: Minimum group size: 10
Adults £4.50 / £3.00 garden only, Child £1.00
Facilities: Shop, Plant Sales, Restaurant, Craft Gallery.
Disabled Access: Partial. Toilet and parking for disabled on site. Wheelchairs on loan, booking necessary.
Tours/Events: A wide variety of events await, please check website for details.
Coach Parking: Yes but limited.
Length of Visit: 4 - 6 hours
Booking Contact: Heather Chislett
Brantwood, Coniston, Cumbria, LA21 8AD
Telephone: 01539 441396   Fax: 01539 441263
Email: heather@brantwood.org.uk
Website: www.brantwood.org.uk
Location: 2 1/4 miles east of Coniston. signposted from Coniston.

Please quote this guide when booking

The Terraces which run down from the southern and western sides of the house are 17th century, though the steps and walls were designed by William Sawrey Gilpin and Anthony Salvin in the 1820s. The clipped yews are late 19th century, reflecting the Arts and Crafts revival of interest in topiary.

The Low Garden was a formal rhododendron garden laid out in 1870. The design of the paths is based on the form of two interlocking stars.

In the 17th century the Walled Garden on the north side of the house was an ornamental Dutch Garden. The walls were built by Henry Fletcher in 1736 and there are records of a large number of fruit trees which were planted then. In the last few years an increasing collection of herbaceous plants has transformed the Walled Garden into a beautiful summer garden.

The Woodland Walk surrounding the gardens includes 65 types of tree and a 17th century dovecote.

Fact File

Opening Times: Gardens: 11am -5am daily (except Saturdays) - 12th April - 31st October 2006.
House: 12.30-4.00 Wed, Thurs, Sun, B.H Mon. 12th April - 1st October 2006.

Admission Rates: Gardens only, Adult £3.50, Senior Citizen £3.50, Child £1.00.
House & Garden Adult £5.50, Child £3.00. Family £15.00

Groups Rates: Minimum group size: 20
Gardens only. Adult £3.00, House & Garden Adult £5.00.

Facilities: Tearoom, Gift Shop on House open days 11.00am - 4.30pm.

Disabled Access: Partial access (many gravel paths). Parking for disabled on site. Electic Wheelchair available.

Tours/Events: Please call for details.

Coach Parking: Yes

Length of Visit: 1 1/2 Hours (with House 3 hours)

Booking Contact: Edward Thompson
Hutton-in-the-Forest, Penrith, Cumbria, CA11 9TH
Telephone: 017684 84449 Fax: 017684 84571

Email: info@hutton-in-the-forest.co.uk

Website: www.hutton-in-the-forest.co.uk

Location: 2 1/2 miles North West of M6 Junction 41 on B5305 towards Wigton; 6 miles from Penrith.

Please quote this guide when booking

41

Levens Hall & Gardens   Cumbria

Original gardens laid out c.1694 by Monsieur Guillaume Beaumont. Yew trees sculptured into cones, corkscrews, circles and other curious shapes, interspersed with impeccably-clipped box, make Levens Hall's Topiary Gardens unique in Britain. Also a fountain garden, potager and herb garden, a bowling green and the earliest English Ha-Ha. Overlooking the garden is the Elizabethan house which contains a fine collection of Jacobean furniture, plasterwork and panelling.

"Considered to be in the top ten of UK Gardens"
Monty Don

"You can almost hear the old yews gossiping and basking in the frame that has come to them after three centuries of patient posing" Tradescant's Diary (RHS Journal).

Fact File

Opening Times: Sunday 2nd April - Thursday 12th October.
Admission Rates: House & Gardens (Gardens Only) Adults £9.00(£6.00),Child £4.00 (£3.00).
Group Rates: Minimum group size: 20
                       House & Gardens (Gardens only) Adults £7.50(£5.50),Child £3.80 (£2.70).
Facilities: Licensed Restaurant and Tea Rooms, Gift Shop, Plant Sales.
Disabled Access: Yes (Not House). Parking for disabled on site. Wheelchairs on loan, booking necessary.
Tours/Events: None
Coach Parking: Yes
Length of Visit: 2 Hours
Booking Contact: Levens Hall, Kendal, Cumbria LA8 0PD
                       Telephone: 015395 60321 Fax: 015395 60669
Email: houseopening@levenshall.co.uk
Website: www.levenshall.co.uk
Location: Junction 36 of M6, Oxenholme railway station.

Please quote this guide when booking

Muncaster

Set in the dramatic grandeur of the Lakeland Fells, the wild, woodland gardens are home to an incredible collection of rare and beautiful plants. Miles of paths wind through this extra-ordinary scenery, which also provides cover for a varied wildlife population. A great plant-hunting tradition flourishes at Muncaster and many of the plants in the gardens are now highly endangered in their native habitats due to population pressures and deforestation. Thousands of specimens, particularly from China and the Far East, have been grown from seed collected on recent expeditions around the turn of the Third Millennium. British plants too flourish in abundance, and the bluebells in the high woods should not be missed in late April and early May. Gardens evolve and change, and no matter what time of year you visit, there is always something in flower and new discoveries to be made, and the highlight: the view from the Castle and Terrace is truly "Heaven's Gate" as described by John Ruskin, the 19th Century father of the conservation movement.

Fact File

Opening Times: 12th February - 5th November open daily 10.30am. (Main Season)
Gardens open all year except January

Admission Rates: Adults £6.50, Child £4.50, Family £20.00.

Group Rates: Minimum group size: 12
Adults £6.00, Child £3.50.

Facilities: 3 Shops, Cafe, Play Area for children.

Disabled Access: Partial. Toilet and parking for disabled on site. Electric Wheelchair on loan, booking necessary

Tours/Events: Festival of Rhododendrons, Camellias & Azaleas (April - May),
Bluebell Heaven - (April - May), R H S Lecture Saturday 6th May 2005.

Coach Parking: Yes

Length of Visit: 3 1/2 hours

Booking Contact: Joanne Wagstaff
Muncaster Castle, Ravenglass, Cumbria, CA18 1RQ
Telephone: 01229 717614 Fax: 01229 717010

Email: Info@muncaster.co.uk

Website: www.muncaster.co.uk

Location: 1 mile south of Ravenglass.

Please quote this guide when booking

"Nowhere on earth have I ever seen a spot of more perfect and enjoyable beauty" wrote Dr. Thomas Arnold.

Visitors to Williams Wordsworth's most beloved home from 1813 – 1850 can enjoy the languid-lived-in feel of Williams Wordsworth's favourite home as you dent the cushions and compare the family snaps of his descendants with the portraits of the bard. It was here the poet wrote and revised many of his famous poems including the world renowned <u>Daffodils</u> and became Poet Laureate to Queen Victoria.

Walk through the magnificent gardens landscaped by the poet, sit in his summerhouse and enjoy the breathtaking views of Lake Windermere, Rydal Water and the surrounding fells then understand why Wordsworth loved to write here.
"… 'Through primrose tufts, in that green bower,
The periwinkle trailed its wreaths;
And 'tis my faith that every flower
Enjoys the air it breaths'…"
William Wordsworth (Lines written in early Spring)

Special Events
Exclusive garden tours, garden weddings, garden picnic tours, all by special arrangement.

Fact File

Opening Times:	Summer: March to October 9.30am - 5pm, Winter: November to February 10am - 4pm (Closed - Tues in Winter, 8th Jan - 1st Feb and Christmas Day).
Admission Rates:	House & Garden - Adults £5.00, Senior Citizen £4.00 - (includes house & garden guide) Garden only £2.50 (includes garden guide) Child £2.00 5 - 15 yrs.
Groups Rates:	Minimum group size 10 House & Garden - Adults £3.75
Facilities:	Gift Shop.
Disabled Access:	Partial, parking for disabled on site.
Tours/Events:	See special events.
Coach Parking:	Yes
Length of Visit:	1 - 1 1/2 hours.
Booking Contact:	Marian Elkington Rydal Mount & Gardens, Rydal Nr Ambleside, Cumbria, LA22 9LU. Tel: 015394 33002 Fax: 015394 31738
Email:	info@rydalmount.co.uk
Website:	www.rydalmount.co.uk
Location:	1 1/2 miles from Ambleside on the A591 Windermere to Keswick Road. Free Parking.

Please quote this guide when booking

Sizergh Castle, originally built in the Middle Ages by the Strickland family, who still live there today, has magnificent furniture and treasures and is surrounded by a wonderful garden with a lake and superb rock garden. There is also a kitchen garden with vegetables, herbs, cut flowers and soft fruits. All this is set in a 1600 acre estate crossed by public footpaths, providing short walks from the castle to dramatic viewpoints over Morecambe Bay and the Lake District fells.

The imposing castle has an exceptional series of oak-panelled rooms. One of the best rooms is the Inlaid Chamber. Portraits, fine furniture and ceramics collected over the centuries by the family are shown alongside their recent photographs.

Fact File

Opening Times:	2nd April - 29th October 2006 Sunday - Thursday inclusive 12 noon - 5pm Closed Fri/Sat.
Admission Rates:	House & Garden Adults £6.20, Child £3.10. Garden only Adults £4.00 Child £2.00. Family Ticket £15.50. Single parent family ticket £10.00
Group Rates:	Minimum group size: 15 - Adults £5.20.
Facilities:	Gift Shop, Tea Room, Plant Sales.
Disabled Access:	Partial. Toilet and parking for disabled on site, Wheelchairs on loan Booking Advisable
Tours/Events:	Ring for details.
Coach Parking:	Yes.
Length of Visit:	2 1/2 hours.
Booking Contact:	Administrator The National Trust, Sizergh Castle and Garden, Sizergh, Nr Kendal. Cumbria, LA8 8AE Tel: 015395 60951 Fax: 015395 60951
Email:	sizergh@nationaltrust.org.uk
Website:	www.nationaltrust .org.uk
Location:	J 36 of the M6, then A590 Kendal direction. Take Barrow-in-Furness turning off and follow brown signs. From Lake District, follow A591 South M6 direction. Turn off towards Barrow-in-Furness (A590) and follow brown signs.

Please quote this guide when booking

Calke Abbey Gardens   Derbyshire

Created in the late eighteenth century, the gardens feature two distinct landscapes uniquely presented to evoke the atmosphere of faded glory, created as the Calke estate slid into a state of decline in the early 20th century. The Pleasure Grounds provide an informal landscape setting for the Mansion and natural screen to the Walled Garden, which is discovered via a sequence of pathways. The Walled Garden incorporates a nationally important collection of late eighteenth century garden buildings, Gardeners Bothy, Peach House, Orangery, Stove House, Backsheds and Gardeners Tunnel all open to be viewed. The Flower Garden, planted in the mid-nineteenth century 'patchwork' style, includes the last surviving example of an auricular theatre. The Physic Garden displays a wide range of fruit and vegetable varieties and the large four acre Kitchen Garden, now redundant, allows the visitor to wonder at the former grandeur of this magnificent garden.

Fact File

Opening Times: House: 18th Mar- 29th Oct Sat - Wed 12.30 -5.00.
Garden: 18th Mar- 29th Oct Sat - Wed 11.00 -5.00. 29th June - 1st Sept Daily 11.00-5.00.

Admission Rates: House & Garden: Adults £6.80, Children: £3.40, Family £17.00.
Garden: Adults £4.20, Children: £2.10, Family £10.50.

Group Rates: Minimum Groups Size: 15
Adults: £5.80 Children: £2.90

Facilities: Shop, Restaurant, Holiday Cottages.

Disabled Access: Yes. Toilet and parking on site. Wheelchair Loan booking available.

Tours/Events: Morning Private Tour available additional charge £7.50.

Coach Parking: Yes.

Length of Visit: 2 hours.

Booking Contact Property Administrator. The National Trust, Calke Abbey, Ticknall, Derby. DE73 1LE
Telephone: 01332 863822 Fax: 01332 865272

Email: calkeabbey@nationaltrust.org.uk

Website: www.nationaltrust.org.uk

Location: Ten miles south of Derby, off A514 at Ticknall.

Please quote this guide when booking

The eighteenth-century landscape garden and park, leading away from the magnificent Palladian House, was created by the 1st Lord Fortescue in 1730 with temples, follies, ponds and across the valley a Triumphal Arch. At the top of the hill above the house is a Castle (complete with cannons) from which Dartmoor, Exmoor and Lundy Island are visible on a clear day. The spring woodland garden shelters magnolias, camellias, rhododendrons, azaleas, a 2 acre daffodil wood, and thousands of bulbs, with some rare and renowned trees in the Easter Close. The summer Millennium garden designed by Xa Tollemache has herbaceous borders planted with lillies, agapanthus, phlox and penstemon edged with box and lavender in gentle curves lining gravel paths plus a spectacular water sculpture by Giles Rayner.

Fact File

Opening Times:	2nd April - 31st August Inc. (every day except Saturday)
Admission Rates:	Adults £4.00, Children under 14 Free.
Group Rates:	None.
Facilities:	Teas in West Wing on Sundays and Bank Holidays. Catering for pre-booked groups.
Disabled Access:	Partial, Toilet and parking for disabled on site.
Tours/Events:	Guided tours £25.00 per guide. Filleigh Fete 19th August 2006.
Coach Parking:	Yes.
Length of Visit:	1 - 2 hours
Booking Contact:	Margaret Pine
	Castle Hill, Filleigh, Barnstaple, Devon, EX32 ORQ
	Telephone: 01598 760336 (Ext 4) Fax: 01598 760457
Email:	ladyarran@castlehill-devon.com
Website:	www.castlehilldevon.co.uk
Location:	Leave A361 at roundabout west of South Molton onto B3226, follow signs to Filleigh. Shortly after passing through Stags Head, yellow lodge on the right. Go through drive gates following signs to car park.

Please quote this guide when booking

Escot Gardens, Maze & Woodland   Devon

Escot is unique. Originally laid out in the 18th century as 220 acres of 'Capability Brown' parkland and gardens, contemporary design elements have been added by Ivan Hicks, the well-known TV gardener-artist. In between, generations of the Kennaway family have travelled the world bringing a wide range of shrubs and magnificent champion trees. Woodland paths and trails now lead visitors to the remarkable new Beech Hedge Maze with its five hedge-leaping bridges and stunning central look-out tower; to the birds of prey with their summertime displays; through the beginnings of an International Tree Foundation wood, carpeted with beautiful flowers in Spring; through the wild boar and otter enclosures; to an award-winning aquatic centre and a dedicated wetlands conservation area.

As a final stop, the Coach House offers a 'House of Marbles' gift shop and a Restaurant which serves delicious home-cooked food using the very best local produce.

Escot is refreshingly uncommercial and, indeed, unique.

Fact File

Opening Times: All year except 25th & 26th December

Admission Rates: Adults £5.50, Senior Citizen £4.00, Child £4.00 (3-15yrs) under 3yrs Free.

Groups Rates: Minimum group size: 10
Adults £5.00, Senior Citizen £3.50, Child £3.50 (3-15yrs) under 3yrs Free.

Facilities: Gift Shop, Plant Sales, Teas, Restaurant, Aquatic & Pet Centre, Maze, Birds of Prey displays, International Tree Foundation Wood, West Country Rivers Trust Demonstration Site, Dedicated Wetlands Conservation Area.

Disabled Access: Partial. Toilet and parking for disabled on site.

Tours/Events: Please call for details.

Coach Parking: Yes

Length of Visit: 3 - 4 Hours + meals

Booking Contact: Mr & Mrs J-M Kennaway (Owners)
Escot, Ottery St Mary, Devon, EX11 1LU.
Telephone: 01404 822188 Fax: 01404 822903

Email: info@escot-devon.co.uk

Website: www.escot-devon.co.uk

Location: See Website for Map - Escot is just off the A30 Exeter to Honiton road at Fairmile. (Follow brown signs).

Please quote this guide when booking

Marwood Hill Gardens   Devon

Created by Dr. Jimmy Smart – a fine plantsman. Marwood Hill has 20 acres of beautiful gardens and three small lakes set in a sheltered valley setting. A haven for trees and shrubs from around the world as well as herbaceous and alpine plants giving all year round interest and colour. The gardens are well known for the extensive collection of Camellias and National Collections of Astilbe, Japanese Iris and Tulbaghia. There are many areas where the visitor can rest, experience the tranquillity and enjoy the many inspiring aspects of the gardens.

The walled garden plant centre sells a wide range of plants, most of which have been grown and propagated in the gardens. Knowledgeable staff are usually available to help and advise.

The Garden Tearoom overlooking the garden offers a selection of light lunches, home baked cakes and Devon cream teas.

Fact File

Opening Times: Gardens: Daily except Christmas Day 9.30 – 5.30, Plant Centre: March – October, Garden Tea Room: March – October

Admission Rates: Adult: £4.00, Children: Under 12 free.

Group Rates: Minimum Groups Size: 15. By appointment only. Adult: £3.50, including introductory talk by Head Gardener.

Facilities: Plant Centre and Garden Tea Room.

Disabled Access: Yes, but limited. Toilet and car parking on site.

Tours/Events: Guided tours available. Contact the booking office for details.

Coach Parking: Yes

Length of Visit: 2 hours – all day.

Booking Contact Mrs. Patricia Stout
Marwood Hill Gardens, Marwood, Barnstaple, North Devon EX31 4EB
Telephone 01271 342528 Fax: 01271 342528

Email: marwoodhillgardens@netbreeze.co.uk

Website: www.marwoodhillgarden.co.uk

Location: 9 miles from Ilfracombe. 4 miles north of Barnstaple.

Please quote this guide when booking

Come and see this enchanting 65-acre garden set in the beautiful Torridge Valley. Whatever the season, Rosemoor is a unique place that people return to time and again for ideas, inspiration or simply to enjoy a relaxing day out.

From Lady Anne's original garden to rose gardens (with over 200 varieties), formal and informal gardens, the fruit and vegetable garden, the arboretum, stunning lake and cottage garden, as well as woodland walks, there is something for everyone to enjoy.

Over 70 exciting events are also held at Rosemoor throughout the year, such as art exhibitions and workshops, horticultural lectures and walks, family events, craft fairs, and musical events. For information, please ring 01805 624067 for a FREE brochure.

Licensed Restaurant, Tea Room, Plant Centre and Shop also on site and free parking.

Fact File

Opening Times: April - September 10am - 6pm, October - March 10am - 5pm, open every day except Christmas Day. Visitor Centre Closed noon Christmas eve and re-opens 10am 27th Dec.

Admission Rates: Adults £5.50, Senior Citizen £5.50, Child (6-16yrs) £1.50, (under 6yrs Free), RHS Members + 1 Guest Free

Group Rates: Minimum group size: 10
Adults £4.50, Senior Citizen £4.50, Child £1.50.

Facilities: Visitor Centre, Shop, Restaurant, Wisteria Tea Room, Plant Centre.

Disabled Access: Yes. Toilet and Parking for disabled on site. Wheelchairs on loan, booking necessary.

Tours/Events: Full programme of events throughout the year.

Coach Parking: Yes

Length of Visit: Half to full day.

Booking Contact: Admin Department
RHS Garden Rosemoor, Great Torrington, North Devon, EX38 8PH
Telephone 01805 624067 Fax: 01805 624717

Email: rosemooradmin@rhs.org.uk

Website: www.rhs.org.uk/rosemoor

Location: 1 mile south of Torrington on the A3124 (formerly B3220)

Please quote this guide when booking

Abbotsbury Sub Tropical Gardens Dorset

Established in 1765 by the first Countess of Ilchester. Developed since then into a 20-acre grade 1 listed magnificent woodland valley garden. world famous for it's Camellia Groves, Magnolias, Rhododendron and Hydrangea collections. In summer it is awash with colour.

Since the restoration after the great storm of 1990 many new and exotic plants have been introduced. The garden is now a mixture of formal and informal, with a charming walled garden and spectacular woodland valley views.

Facilities include a Colonial Tea House for lunches, snacks and drinks, a Plant Centre and quality Gift Shop. Events such as Shakespeare and concerts are presented during the year. The Floodlighting of the Garden at the end of October (Oct 18th - Nov 5th 2006) should not be missed.

Fact File

Opening Times:	Summer: 10am - 6pm last entry at 5pm.
	Winter (November - February) - 10.00am - 4pm or dusk, last entry 1 hour before.
Admission Rates:	Adults £7.50, Senior Citizen £7.00, Child £4.50
Groups Rates:	Minimum group size 10
	Adults £6.00, Senior Citizen £5.50, Child £3.50
Facilities:	Colonial Tea House, Gift Shop, Plant Centre.
Disabled Access:	Yes. 50% of garden accessible. Toilet and parking for disabled on site. Wheelchairs F.O.C.
Tours/Events:	£1 per person (minimum charge £20) on top of the group rate (minimum 10 people).
	Special events see web site.
Coach Parking:	Yes
Length of Visit:	2 hours
Booking Contact:	Jess Owen. Abbotsbury Sub Tropical Garden, Bullers Way, Abbotsbury, (Nr Weymouth), Dorset, DT3 4LA. Telephone: 01305 871130 Fax: 01305 871092
Email:	info@abbotsbury-tourism.co.uk
Website:	www.abbotsbury-tourism.co.uk
Location:	On the B3157 between Weymouth and Bridport in Dorset. come off the A35 near Dorchester at Winterborne Abbas.

Please quote this guide when booking

Laid out by successive members of the Bankes family over the last three centuries, the grounds of this extensive estate are presented by the National Trust in their Edwardian splendour. Most recent of the restoration projects is the Japanese Gardens of Henrietta Bankes, the formal Tea Gardens of which were opened in 2005, set in seven acres of the southern shelter-belt and include an Acer Glade, a Quarry Garden, an Evergreen Garden and a Cherry Garden.

Closer to the magnificent Mansion are the Sunk Garden and the Parterre, both of which remain true to their early twentieth century planting patterns throughout the year. The Fernery, with over thirty-five varieties, is also the home of the National Collection of Anemone nemorosa, while the surrounding three hundred-acre Parkland reflects the Bankes' passion for specimen trees whether as single examples or as groups and avenues.

Fact File

Opening Times:	18th March – 29th October: Daily 10.30 a.m. – 6 p.m.
	3rd November – 17th December: Friday, Saturday and Sunday: 10.30 a.m. – 4 p.m.
Admission Rates:	Gardens Only: Adults: £4.50, Children: £2.30.
Group Rates:	Minimum Groups Size: 15
	Group rates for House and Gardens only: Adults: £7.50, Children: £3.80.
Facilities:	Woodland Walks, Children's play areas.
Disabled Access:	Yes – gardens only. Toilet and car parking on site. Wheelchair Loan booking available.
Tours/Events:	Guided tours available. Events leaflet available.
Coach Parking:	Yes – booking essential.
Length of Visit:	2 hours +
Booking Contact	Carol Dougherty, Property Administrator
	Kingston Lacy, Wimborne Minster, Dorset BH21 4EA
	Telephone: 01202 883402 Fax: 01202 882402
Email:	kingstonlacy@nationaltrust.org.uk
Website:	www.nationaltrust.org.uk
Location:	1 1/2 miles west of Wimborne Minster, on B3082.

Please quote this guide when booking

Kingston Maurward Gardens & Animal Park   Dorset

The contemporary parkland and pleasure gardens were laid out in the "Jardin Anglais" style popularised by Capability Brown, which consisted of rolling turf, carefully placed groups of trees and a lake. The lovely 35 acre formal gardens were created between 1915 and 1922 within the existing framework of the 18th Century Parkland setting. The gardens have undergone an extensive programme of restoration with new plantings rich in variety and interest. Gardens are not static and Kingston Maurward, like all good gardens, is constantly evolving.

The Animal Park is a firm favourite with children and home to an interesting collection of animals. There is a large play area and plenty of space for picnics. The Visitor Centre provides information on the Animal Park and Gardens and has a wide variety of plants and gifts for sale.

Fact File

Opening Times:	4th January 2006 to 21st December 10am - 5.30pm.
Admission Rates:	Adults £5.00, Senior Citizen £4.50, Child £3.00, Family £15.50.
Group Rates:	Minimum group size: 10
	Adults £4.50, Senior Citizen £4.50, Child £3.00.
Facilities:	Visitor Centre, Shop, Tea Room, Plant Sales, Picnic Area
	Children's Play Area, Animal Park.
Disabled Access:	Yes. Toilet & parking for disabled on site. Wheelchairs on loan, booking necessary.
Tours/Events:	Guided walks are available if booked in advance.
	Special events take place throughout the year, telephone for details.
Coach Parking:	Yes
Length of Visit:	Minimum 2 hours
Booking Contact:	Ginny Rolls
	Kingston Maurward, Dorchester, Dorset, DT2 8PY
	Telephone 01305 215003 Fax: 01305 215001
Email:	events@kmc.ac.uk
Website:	www.kmc.ac.uk/gardens
Location:	Signposted from the roundabout at the eastern end of the Dorchester by-pass A35.

Please quote this guide when booking

Minterne, described by Simon Jenkins as 'a corner of paradise', was landscaped after the manner of Capability Brown in the 18th Century with small lakes and cascades. The first Himalayan Rhododendrons were planted in the 1850s, followed by many more from the Himalayan expeditions of George Forrest, Wilson & Rock around 1905, and from Kingdon Ward's expeditions in the 1920's.

Wander peacefully through 20 wild woodland acres of hidden gardens laid out in a horseshoe over a mile round; March sees the magnolias and early rhododendrons, April and May, Japanese cherries and a profusion of Rhododendrons and azaleas, together with Pieris Forrestii with its brilliant red shoots. In late May and June many fine specimens of Davidia Involucrata (the pocket handkerchief tree) are a particular feature. Eucryphias, Hydrangeas, water plants and water lilies provide a new vista at each turn. The autumn colouring is quite sensational. Home to the Churchill and Digby families for 350 years, the house with many Churchill pictures and tapestries is open for organised groups only. Contact 01300 341370.

Fact File

Opening Times:	Daily 1st March – 31st October, 10 a.m. – 6 p.m.
Admission Rates:	Adults: £4.00, Children free.
Group Rates:	By prior appointment.
Facilities:	Picnic facilities in the car park.
Disabled Access:	Yes, limited. Toilet and car parking on site.
Tours/Events:	Guided house and garden tours available by appointment.
Coach Parking:	Yes.
Length of Visit:	$1^1/_2$ - 2 hours.
Booking Contact	Maureen Panchen or Sophie Digby
	Minterne Gardens, Minterne Magna, Dorchester, Dorset DT2 7AU
	Telephone: 01300 341370 Fax: 01300 341747
Email:	enquiries@minterne.co.uk
Website:	www.minterne.co.uk
Location:	On A352 Dorchester to Sherborne Road, 2 miles north of Cerne Abbas, Dorset.

Please quote this guide when booking

Stapehill is a superb venue for group visits, offering a wide range of attractions to suit people of all tastes and ages for one admission price. The glorious award winning gardens, including the stunning Japanese Garden stocked with beautiful koi carp are a joy to behold. The 12,000 sq.ft museum with it's artisan workshops tells the history of farming through Victorian England. The 19th Century Cistercian Abbey houses the crafts people and has the Nuns Chapel, Cloisters and Cloister Garden plus the history of the Abbey, all this creates a truly unique experience, and with all but the gardens under cover, even the weather cannot spoil a memorable day at Stapehill.

The lovely licensed coffee shop provides morning coffee, light lunches, afternoon, and cream teas. Special events are held throughout the year including craft fairs, flower and garden festival and our magical Christmas weekends.

Fact File

Opening Times: Daily 10am - 5pm Easter - September. Wednesday - Sunday 10am - 4pm October - Easter. Closed Christmas Holiday and all of January.

Admission Rates: Adults £7.50, Senior Citizen £7.00, Child £4.50

Groups Rate: Minimum group size: 15
Adults £6.00, Senior Citizen £5.50, Child £4.00

Facilities: Visitor Centre, Shop, Plant Sales, Teas, Licensed Coffee Shop with home-made quiches and other light lunches.

Disabled Access: Yes. Toilet and Parking for disabled on site.

Tours/Events: All year - please call for details

Coach Parking: Yes

Length of Visit: 2 1/2 plus hours (all weather attraction)

Booking Contact: Mrs Sheena Tinsdale. Stapehill Abbey, 276 Wimborne Road West, Stapehill, Wimborne, Dorset, BH21 2EB. Telephone: 01202 861686   Fax: 01202 894589

Email: None

Website: None

Location: 2 1/2 miles east of the Historic town of Wimborne Minster.
Just off A31 at Canford Bottom roundabout.

Please quote this guide when booking

Enter the Tudor Walled Garden at Cressing Temple and you step back in time. The plants that grow here are those that would have been available in the Tudor period; the design, a result of painstaking research and archaeological excavation.

Within the Tudor walls of the Garden are themed areas, with borders devoted to medicinal, culinary and dyers' plants, a potager and nuttery. The nosegay garden is a fragrant delight with its wealth of sweetly scented plants, grown in the period for their perfume. The arbour is planted to recall Shakespeare's Midsummer Night's Dream with a profusion of roses, woodbine and oxlips.

The Walled Garden nestles to the side of one of the two magnificent medieval Barns for which Cressing Temple is renowned. These date to the early 13th century, a time when the site was owned by the mysterious Knights Templar.

Fact File

Opening Times: Daily March - October (except Saturday) 10am - 4.30pm Last entry 3.30pm

Admission Rates: Adults £3.50, Senior Citizen £2.50, Child £2.50 (under 3yrs free). Family (2+3) £8.50.

Group Rates: 10% discount on groups over 15

Facilities: Gift shop, Plant Sales, Tea Room, Medieval Barns & Exhibition. Audio Guide, Tour guides Sundays or on request.

Disabled Access: Yes. Toilet and parking for disabled on site. Wheelchairs on loan.

Tours/Events: Various events through the year, for details call or see our website.

Coach Parking: Yes

Length of Visit: 1 1/2 - 2 hours

Booking Contact: Colleen Coles, Witham Road, Braintree, Essex, CM77 8PD
Telephone: 01376 584903 Fax: 01376 584864

Email: cressing.temple@essexcc.gov.uk

Website: www.cressingtemple.org.uk

Location: From A12 take Witham turn off, then follow signs to Braintree, Cressing Temple is on the B1018. From A120 follow brown signs towards Freeport, Cressing Temple is sign posted.

Please quote this guide when booking

The Gibberd Garden   Essex

The garden is a highly individual creation of Sir Frederick Gibberd, Master planner for Harlow new town. It is sited on the side of a small valley which slopes down to a brook. Occupying some seven acres, the garden was planned as a series of 'rooms', each with its own character. The glades, pools and alleys provide settings for some fifty sculptures, large ceramic pots, architectural salvage, a gazebo and even a children's moated castle with a drawbridge! Jane Brown, the garden and landscape design writer, has described it as "one of the few outstanding examples of 20th Century garden design".

The Gibberd Garden Trust aims to realise Sir Frederick's wish that the garden sould be open to the public for study and relaxation. It has been acquired with the generous help of the Heritage Lottery Fund and is currently undergoing an imaginative and extensive restoration programme.

Fact File

Opening Times:	2pm to 6pm Wednesdays, Saturdays, Sundays & Bank Holidays. Beginning April to end September.
Admission Rates:	Adults £4.00, Concessions £2.50, Child Free if accompanied
Group Rates:	Minimum group size: 10 (As above during open times) Please telephone for details at other times.
Facilities:	Visitor Centre, Shop, Teas.
Disabled Access:	Restricted. Toilet and parking for disabled on site.
Tours/Events:	None.
Coach Parking:	Please telephone to make arrangements (restricted access, 33 seater only).
Length of Visit:	2 hours
Booking Contact:	Mrs Jane Quinton The Gibberd Garden, Marsh Lane, Gilden Way, Harlow, Essex, CM17 0NA Telephone: 01279 442112
Email:	enquiries@thegibberdgarden.co.uk
Website:	www.thegibberdgarden.co.uk
Location:	Off B183 Harlow to Hatfield Heath Road. Brown Signs.

Please quote this guide when booking

RHS Garden Hyde Hall

Situated in the heart of Essex farmland in Rettendon to the south of Chelmsford, RHS Garden Hyde Hall is the perfect place to discover the real Essex. With countryside views so rarely associated with this part of England, Hyde Hall is a palate of sumptuous rich and varied colours providing inspiration for the novice and keen gardener alike. Just 40 miles from London, this haven of peace and tranquillity provides the perfect day out. Now open all year round, recent work in the garden has focused on introducing planting and design that will captivate and inspire visitors throughout the seasons.

Throughout the year an extensive range of courses, workshops and special events are organised, with the aim of both enriching a visit to the garden, but also to encourage adults and children to try their hand at something new. The thriving schools programme provides education for any age group, the onsite Education Officer working with teachers to cover a range of subjects linked to the National Curriculum.

Fact File

Opening Times:	**Now open all year** (except for Christmas Day) 10am to 6pm (5pm or dusk Oct - Mar) Last entry one hour before closing.
Admission Rates:	Adults £5.00, Child (6-16) £1.00. RHS member + one guest free.
Groups Rates:	Minimum group size 10 + pre-booked Adults £3.50 - RHS member + one guest free. (Free meal voucher for coach driver)
Facilities:	Plant Centre & Gift Shop, Licensed Barn Restaurant, Visitor Centre, Garden Library.
Disabled Access:	Most areas. Parking, toilet facilities and ramped access to Barn Restaurant.
Tours/Events:	Contact garden direct for a copy of the Events Programme or visit the website.
Coach Parking:	Yes
Length of Visit:	3 - 4 hours
Booking Contact:	Group Bookings Administrator, RHS Garden Hyde Hall, Buckhatch Lane, Rettendon, Chelmsford, Essex CM3 8ET. Telephone : 01245 400256 Fax; 01245 402100
Email:	hydehall@rhs.org.uk Website: www.rhs.org.uk
Location:	South-east of Chelmsford, Brown tourism signed from A130.

Please quote this guide when booking

The newly redesigned Walled Garden at Marks Hall was greeted with great enthusiasm when it opened in 2003.

The five individual gardens and the double long border are a unique blend of traditional and contemporary, combining unusual landscaping and creative and colourful planting. This garden is at its best from early summer through to autumn but on the opposite lake bank there is the Millennium Walk designed to be at its best in the shortest days of the year. Here the stems of dogwood, rubus and birch reflect in the lake and the scent of Hamamelis lingers.

There is much more to see in this Aboretum and Garden of over 100 acres and new plantings mature and surprise each year.

Fact File

Opening Times:	Tuesday - Sunday 10.30am - 5pm, Bank Holdiays and winter weekends.
Admission Rates:	£4.50 per car. £2.50 per person.
Groups Rates:	Minimum group size 12
	£2.00 per person
Facilities:	Visitor Centre, Shop, Plant Sales, Teas Restaurant.
Disabled Access:	Yes. Toilet and parking for disabled on site. Wheelchairs and buggy on loan.
Tours/Events:	Please telephone for details.
Coach Parking:	Yes
Length of Visit:	2 1/2 hours
Booking Contact:	Visitor Centre Manager
	Marks Hall, Coggeshall, Essex, CO6 1TG
	Tel: 01376 563796 Fax: 01376 563132
Email:	enquiries@markshall.org.uk
Website:	www.markshall.org.uk
Location:	Signed from A120 Coggeshall by-pass.

Please quote this guide when booking

Batsford Arboretum & Wild Garden   Gloucestershire

Batsford Arboretum & Wild Garden - The Cotswolds Secret Garden and former home of the Mitford family.

One of the largest private collection of trees in Great Britain. See spring flowers as they cascade down the hillside. Many wild orchids and fritillaries adorn the arboretum. In autumn the many rare and unusual trees explode into their magnificent reds, golds and purples.

Follow the stream through pools and waterfalls to its source, make a wish with the giant Buddha. find the Foo Dog hidden amongst the trees, then negotiate the waterfall without getting too wet. See if you can find Algernon and Clemantine on the lake, then rest awhile and view the deer in the Deer Park. Fifty acres of peace, traquillity - pure Cotswold magic!

Fact File

Opening Times: 10am - 5pm 1st February - 15th November.
Week-ends only from 15th November - 1st February.
Also open Boxing day & New Years Day.

Admission Rates: Adults £6.00, Senior Citizen £5.00, Child £2.00.

Groups Rates: Minimum group size 20. Admission Rates less 10%

Facilities: Visitor Centre, Shop, Plant Sales, Teas, Restaurant, Garden Centre and Falconry Centre.

Disabled Access: Partial. Toilet and parking for disabled on site, wheelchairs on loan, booking necessary.

Tours/Events: Tours by arrangement. Events to be arranged.

Coach Parking: Yes new area.

Length of Visit: 2 Hours

Booking Contact: Mr Chris Pilling
Batford Arboretum, Batsford Park, Moreton in Marsh, Glos GL56 9QB.
Telephone: 01386 701441 Fax: 01386 701829

Email: batsarb@batsfound.freeserve.co.uk

Website: www.batsarb.co.uk

Location: 1 mile east of Moreton in Marsh on A44 road.

Please quote this guide when booking

Bourton House Garden   Gloucestershire

Intensively planted, this 3-acre garden features excitingly planted herbaceous borders full of stunning plant and colour combinations.

Neatly clipped box and yew is found in knots, parterres and spiralling topiary. Water wends it way through small fountains, pools and ponds. A sub-tropical border, raised alpine troughs, a shadehouse, all provide further variety in this continually evolving garden, and add to the whole, a myriad of magically planted pots and containers.

Planted less than 10 years ago with a wide variety of trees, the seven-acre field opposite already boasts some sizeable specimens.

The imposing 16th century Tithe barn now houses a gallery of contemporary Art, Craft and Design.

Fact File

Opening Times:	24th May - 31st August: Wednesday, Thursday & Friday. September - 27th October: Thursday & Friday. 10am - 5pm.
Admission Rates:	Adults £5.00, Senior Citizen £4.50, Child Free.
Groups Rates:	Minimum group size 20 Adults £4.50.
Facilities:	Gallery of Contemporary Art, Craft, Design in the Tithe Barn, Teas & Light Meals until mid September. Plants for sale.
Disabled Access:	There is limited access for wheelchairs: 70%
Tours/Events:	Please see website for current activities.
Coach Parking:	Yes
Length of Visit:	1 1/2 hours
Booking Contact:	Monique B Paice Bourton House, Bourton-On-The-Hill, Moreton-in-Marsh, Glos, GL56 9AE Tel: 01386 700121 Fax: 01386 701081
Email:	cd@bourtonhouse.com
Website:	www.bourtonhouse.com
Location:	2 miles west of Moreton-in Marsh on the A44.

Please quote this guide when booking

Cerney House Gardens   Gloucestershire

Cerney House Gardens are a romantic, secret step back into the past. Set amongst parkland, this family-run estate bulges with old-fashioned splendour. The central walled garden boasts a working kitchen garden complemented with generous herbaceous borders and roses of every description. A quieter knot garden plays host to the annual 'Floral Fireworks' tulip festival. There is a well-labelled herb garden that leads to the woodland, which is carpeted in the spring with snowdrops followed by bluebells. The avenue beds lead to genera borders that map out plant connections and end in turn amongst the ever-growing arboretum. There are plant collections throughout, including the national collection of Tradescantia. The air is full of scents and nature's sounds. But this is still essentially a family garden where your guide will often be one of the many resident pets.

Fact File

Opening Times: Easter to end of July or by appointment. Open: Tuesday, Wednesday, Friday, Sunday.
Admission Rates: Adults: £3.00, Children: £1.00.
Group Rates: Adults: £3.00, organiser entrance free, Children: £1.00
Facilities: Shop, Plant Sales, Teas, Pottery.
Disabled Access: Yes. Toilet and car parking on site. Wheelchair loan available please book.
Tours/Events: Guided tours available. Annual Tulip Festival.
Coach Parking: By arrangement.
Length of Visit: 1 1/2 hours
Booking Contact   Barbara McPherson
       Cerney House Gardens, North Cerney, Cirencester, Gloucestershire GL7 7BX
       Telephone 01285 831300/831205   Fax: 01285 831421
Email: barbara@cerneygardens.com
Website: www.cerneygardens.com
Location: On the A435 at North Cerney. Turn up behind village church, 400 metres from main road.

Please quote this guide when booking

Hidcote Manor Garden   Gloucestershire

Hidcote Manor Garden is one of Englands's great Arts and Craft gardens. Created by the American horticulturist Major Lawrence Johnston in 1907, Hidcote is famous for its rare trees and shrubs, outstanding herbaceous borders and unusual plants from all over the world.

The garden is divided by tall hedges and walls to create a series of outdoor 'rooms' each with its own special and unique character. From the formal splendour of the White Garden and Bathing Pool to the informality and beauty of the Old Garden, visitors are assured of a surprise around every corner.

The numerous outdoor rooms reach their height at different times of the year, making a visit to Hidcote Manor Garden enjoyable whatever the season.

Fact File

Opening Times: 25 March - 29 October: Monday, Tuesday, Wednesday, Saturday & Sunday 10.30am - 6pm (last admission 5pm). From October last admission 4pm.

Admission Rates: Adults £7.00, Senior Citizen £7.00, Child £3.50. (National Trust members free)

Groups Rates: Minimum group size: 15
Adults £6.20, Senior Citizen £6.20, Child £3.10 (National Trust members free)

Facilities: Shop, Plant Centre, Teas & Restaurant.

Disabled Access: Partial. Toilet and parking for disabled on site. Wheelchairs on loan.

Tours/Events: Please contact the property for a list of special events.

Coach Parking: Yes. Groups must book in advanced.

Length of Visit: 2 hours

Booking Contact: Lisa Edinborough,
Hidcote Manor Garden, Hidcote Bartrim, Chipping Campden, Gloucestershire, GL55 6LR
Telephone: 01386 438333   Fax: 01386 438817

Email: hidcote@nationaltrust.org.uk

Website: www.nationaltrust.org.uk/hidcote

Location: 4 miles north east of Chipping Campden; 8 miles south of Stratford Upon Avon & signposted from B4632 Stratford/Broadway road, close to the village of Mickleton.

Please quote this guide when booking

Kiftsgate is a glorious garden to visit throughout the seasons with spectacular views to the Malvern Hills and beyond. Three generations of women gardeners have designed, planted and sustained this garden.

The upper gardens around the house are planted to give harmonious colour schemes, whilst the sheltered lower gardens recreate the atmosphere of warmer countries. The latest addition is a modern water garden which provides an oasis of tranquillity and contrast to the exuberance of the flower gardens.

On open days plants grown from the garden are for sale. A wide and interesting selection are always available. The tearoom in the house offers delicous home made cream teas and light lunches in June and July.

"Winner of the HHA/Christies Garden of the Year award 2003"

Fact File

Opening Times: May, June & July - Monday, Tuesday, Wednesday, Saturday & Sunday 12noon - 6pm.
April, August & September - Sunday, Monday & Wednesday, 2pm - 6pm.

Admission Rates: Adults £5.50, Senior Citizen £5.50, Child £1.50

Groups Rates: Coaches by appointment, 20 adults or more £5.00 per person

Facilities: Plants for Sale, Tea Room.

Disabled Access: No

Tours/Events: None

Coach Parking: Yes.

Length of Visit: 1 1/2 hours

Booking Contact: Mrs Anne Chambers
Kiftsgate Court Garden, Chipping Campden, Gloucestershire, GL55 6LN
Telephone: 01386 438777   Fax: 01386 438777

Email: kiftsgte@aol.com

Website: www.Kiftsgate.co.uk

Location: 3 miles north east of Chipping Campden. Follow signs towards Mickleton, then follow brown tourist signs to Kiftsgate Court Gardens.

Please quote this guide when booking

Lydney Park Spring Gardens   Gloucestershire

A place of tranquil beauty amidst fine formal gardens, Lydney Park is home to Viscount Bledisloe, and is steeped in history from Iron Age to the present day. In early season, the visitor to Lydney Park drives between a resplendent display of daffodils and narcissi, and beyond the car park are the Spring Gardens, a secret wooded valley with lakes, providing a profusion of Rhododendrons, Azaleas and other flowering shrubs. Discover an important Roman Temple Site and the site of a Normal Castle. Picnic in the Deer Park amongst some magnificent trees, and visit our museums, which includes a New Zealand Museum. Home made teas in Dining Room of House. Dogs welcome on leads.

Fact File

Opening Times:	26th March - 4th June, Sun, Wed & Bank Hol Monday. Daily 30th April - 7th May and 28th May - 4th June.
Admission Rates:	Adults £4.00 (Wed £3.00) Senior Citizen £4.00, Child 50p,
Groups Rate:	Minimum group size: 25 - Phone for group rates.
Facilities:	Tea Rooms, Roman Temple Site, Museums, Gift Shop, Plant Sales.
Disabled Access:	Partial. Parking for disabled on site.
Tours/Events:	Tour of Garden can be made available.
Coach Parking:	Yes
Length of Visit:	1 - 2 hours
Booking Contact:	Sally James
	Lydney Park Gardens, Lydney Park, Estate Office, Old Park, Lydney, Gloucestershire, GL15 6BU.
	Telephone: 01594 842844 Fax: 01594 842027
Email:	sally_lydneypark@btconnect.com
Website:	None
Location:	Situated off A48 between Chepstow and Gloucester.

Please quote this guide when booking

This lovely timeless English Garden, which commands spectacular views over the Golden Valley has most of the features one would expect a garden started in the 17th century. There are extensive yew hedges and a notable yew walk dividing the walled garden, the york stone terrace, the Lutyens Loggia overhung with Wisteria, and a good specimen of magnolia sulangiana. The south lawn supports splendid grass steps and a fine mulburry (probably planted when the original house was built in 1620). West of the house the ground ascends in a series of lawns, terraces and shrubberies. Within the walled garden are two good herbaceous borders, amongst the longest in the country. The walls are planted with climbing and rambler roses and there is a rose pergola dividing the border. A rill with a fountain and the stone summer-house were added as a feature to mark the new Millennium. More recently a circular parterre has been established with tulips, alliums, hebes and lavender. There are many fine specimen trees and the spring show of blossom and bulbs is notable.

Fact File

Opening Times: 10am - 5pm, Tuesday, Wednesday & Thursday, 1st April - 30th September.
Admission Rates: Adults £4.00, Senior Citizen £4.00, Child Free
Group Rates: Minimum group size: 20
Adults £3.60, Senior Citizen £3.60, Child Free
Facilities: Nurseries Adjacent.
Disabled Access: Yes. Parking for disabled on site.
Tours/Events: None.
Coach Parking: Yes
Length of Visit: 1 1/2 hours
Booking Contact: Major M.T.N.H. Wills
Misarden Park, Miserden, Stroud, Glos, GL6 7JA
Telephone 01285 821303 Fax: 01285 821530
Email: estate.office@miserdenestate.co.uk
Website: None
Location: Follow signs to Miserden from A417 or from B4070.

Please quote this guide when booking

Historic formal hillside garden, Stuart period. The Tudor Manor house (1450-1616), garden and outbuildings lie in a picturesque wooded setting under the Cotswold hills.

The terraced garden is a rare survival of an early formal garden on a manorial scale, re-ordered in 1723, with magnificent yew topiary, old roses and box parterres. After being uninhabited for over 100 years, it was restored sympathetically in 'Old English' style by Norman Jewson in 1926.

Fact File

Opening Times:	2nd May to 29th September, Tuesdays, Thursday and Sundays, Gardens and Restaurant 12.00 noon - 5.00pm. House 2pm - 5pm.
Admission Rates:	Garden Only - Adults £3.25, Senior Citizen £3.25, Child £1.25 House & Garden - Adults £5.25, Senior Citizen £5.25, Child £2.25
Groups Rates:	Minimum group size: 25 Adults £4.75, Senior Citizen £4.75, Child £2.25
Facilities:	Restaurant, Lunches and Teas.
Disabled Access:	No. Parking for disabled on site.
Tours/Events:	None.
Coach Parking:	Yes.
Length of Visit:	1 1/2 - 2 hours
Booking Contact:	Jayne Simmons, Owlpen Estate Office Owlpen Manor, Uley, Dursley, Gloucestershire, GL11 5BZ Telephone: 01453 860261 Fax: 01453 860819
Email:	sales@owlpen.com
Website:	www.owlpen.com
Location:	1/2 mile east off B4066 at village green in Uley, between Dursley and Stroud.

Please quote this guide when booking

Painswick Rococo Garden   Gloucestershire

Painswick Rococo Garden is a fascinating insight into 18th century English garden design. The only complete Rococo garden in England, it dates from a brief period (1720-1760) when English gardens where changing from the formal to the informal. These Rococo gardens combined formal vists with winding woodland walks and more natural planting. However Rococo gardens were so much more, their creators showed off their wealth and included features that were both flamboyant and frivolous. The gardens featured buldings of unusual architectural styles, to be used as both eye catchers and view points. These gardens became regency playrooms, an extension of the house to be enjoyed by the owner and his guests.

We are restoring the Garden back to how it was shown in a painting dated 1748. We have contemporary buidings, woodland walks, herbaceous borders, and a large kitchen garden all hidden away in a charming Cotswold valley with splendid views of the surrounding countryside. Visit our Anniversary Maze.

Fact File

Opening Times:	10th January - 31st October. Daily 11am - 5pm.
Admission Rates:	Adults £5.00, Senior Citizen £4.00, Child £2.50
Groups Rates:	Minimum group size: 20 (includes free introductory talk)
	Adults £4.00, Senior Citizen £3.50
Facilities:	Visitor Centre, Shop, Plant Sales, Teas, Restaurant.
Disabled Access:	No. Toilet for disabled on site.
Tours/Events:	None.
Coach Parking:	Yes.
Length of Visit:	2 hours
Booking Contact:	Paul Moir
	Painswick Rococo Garden, Gloucestershire, GL6 6TH
	Telephone: 01452 813204 Fax: 01452 814888
Email:	prm@rococogarden.co.uk
Website:	www.rococogarden.co.uk
Location:	1/2 mile outside Painswick on B4073

Please quote this guide when booking

Rodmarton Manor is the supreme example of the Cotswold Arts and Crafts Movement. The garden was laid out as the house was being built (1909-1929) as a series of outdoor rooms covering about 8 acres. Each garden room has a different character and is bounded by either walls or hedges. One "garden room" has 26 separate beds with a wide variety of planting dominated by yellow shrubs and roses. There is a collection of stone troughs with alpines as well a rockery with bigger alpines. Topiary is a feature of the garden with extensive yew, box beech and holly hedges and clipped features including some new topiary. The herbaceous borders are magnificent from May but peaking late June but with plenty flowering into September. Many different types of roses flourish in the garden including old fashioned well-scented ones. There is a walled Kitchen Garden which has other plants besides vegetables including trained apples and pears. There is a big snowdrop collection. Most people who visit Rodmarton see the house which has specially made furniture as well as seeing the garden.

Fact File

Opening Times:	12th, 16th, 19th February from 1.30pm, (Garden only for snowdrops). Easter Monday 17th April 2pm - 5pm. Wednesdays, Saturdays, Bank Holidays 1st May - 30th September 2pm - 5pm. Private coach bookings at other times.
Admission Rates:	House and Garden £7.00 (5-15yrs £3.50). Garden only £4.00 (5 - 15yrs £1.00)
Facilities:	Teas
Disabled Access:	Yes. Most of garden and ground floor of house.
Tours/Events:	Guided tours of garden available.
Coach Parking:	Yes
Length of Visit:	2 hours for house and garden
Booking Contact:	Simon Biddulph, Rodmarton Manor, Cirencester, GL7 6PF. Telephone 01285 841253 Fax: 01285 841298
Email:	simon.biddulph@farming.co.uk
Website:	www.rodmarton-manor.co.uk
Location:	Off A433 between Cirencester and Tetbury. (no dogs)

Please quote this guide when booking

Stanway House & Fountain   Gloucestershire

Beautiful Jacobean manor house, parkland, one of the finest water-gardens in England. The magnificent fountain – 300 feet high – making it the tallest garden fountain and gravity fountain in the world.

Stanway has been called "as perfect and pretty a Cotswold manor house as anyone is likely to see" is now complemented by the ongoing restoration of its magnificent landscape garden designed, probably by Charles Bridgeman, in the 1720s.

The 500-foot long Canal, on a terrace above the house, the Pyramid Pond, part of the main Cascade (the longest in Britain), the tufa waterfall and the grasswork were restored in 1998 and last year the single-jet fountain was installed. It is hoped to open the 250-yard-long Upper Cascade and the water-powered corn mill in 2007.

Fact File

Opening Times:	House and Garden, June 2006: Tuesday and Thursday 2.00 – 5.00 p.m.
	House and Garden, July & August 2006: Tuesday and Thursday: 2.00 – 5.00 p.m.
	Garden: Saturday 2.00 – 5.00 p.m.
Admission Rates:	House & Garden/Garden only: Adults: £6.00/£4.00, Senior Citizens: £4.50/£3.00, Children: £1.50/£1.00.
Group Rates:	Minimum Groups Size: 10
	Adults: £4.50/£3.00, Senior Citizens: £4.50/£3.00, Children: £1.50/£1.00.
Facilities:	Teas available. Toilet and car parking on site.
Disabled Access:	No.
Tours/Events:	Guided tours available.
Coach Parking:	Yes.
Length of Visit:	2 hours +
Booking Contact	Debbie Lewis
	Stanway House & Fountain, Stanway House, Stanway, Cheltenham, Glos. GL54 5PQ
	Telephone: 01386 584528 Fax: 01386 584688
Email:	stanwayhse@btopenworld.com
Website:	www.stanwayfountain.co.uk
Location:	B4077 between Toddington and Stow-on-the-Would.

Please quote this guide when booking

Sudeley Castle Gardens & Exhibitions   Gloucestershire

14 acres of glorious, organically managed gardens. Bold areas of planting such as those surrounding the 15th century Tithe Barn ruins contrast with intricate detail as seen in the Tudor Knot Garden. Topiary features strongly throughout and the famous Queens Garden, full of English roses, is furnished on two sides by magnificent double yew hedges planted in 1860. A Victorian Vegetable Garden works with the HDRA to help preserve rare and endangered vegetables. More recent additions include the East Garden, its arbour and beds planted with white wisterias, oriental clematis and tree peonies, and a newly landscaped Pheasantry and Wildfowl area.

Fact File

Opening Times:	Open daily 4th March - 29th October 2006, 10.30am - 5.00pm.
Admission Rates:	Adults £7.20, Concessions £6.20, Children £4.20. Family (2 adults and 2 children) £20.80.
Group Rates:	Group rates available.
Facilities:	Visitor Centre, Plant Sales, Coffee Shop and Picnic Area.
Disabled Access:	Limited - garden only. Toilet and Parking for disabled on site.
Tours/Events:	Guided tours available - must be pre-booked. Special events programme, please call for details. (Information may be subject to change, please call or check website).
Coach Parking:	Yes
Length of Visit:	3 hours
Booking Contact:	Group Bookings
	Sudeley Castle, Winchcombe, Cheltenham, Gloucestershire, GL54 5JD
	Telephone: 01242 602308 Fax: 01242 602959
Email:	enquiries@sudeley.org.uk
Website:	www.sudeleycastle.co.uk
Location:	On B4632, 8 miles north east of Cheltenham.

The Grade I listed gardens of Westonbirt School were designed by Robert Holford (1808-1892), best known as founder of the National Arboretum at Westonbirt. Both the School Gardens and the Arboretum were originally part of the same private estate, with Westonbirt House, now the main school building, at its heart.

The School Gardens include many notable specimen trees as well as extensive terraced 'pleasure grounds', Italianate walled gardens, water features, statuary, a grotto, a grass amphitheatre, and wooded walks to a lake.

Many visitors combine their visit to Westonbirt School Gardens with a trip to the nearby Aboretum and find it fascinating to spot the similarities and differences between the formal, highly architectural School Gardens and the Arboretum. NB The National Arboretum at Westonbirt is now owned and operated by the Forestry Commission and a separate entry charge is payable.

Fact File

Opening Times: Thursday - Sunday only; Sat 25th March - Sun 16th April, Sun 9th July - Sun 10th September Daily; Sun 29th October - Sunday 5th November, Bank Holiday Monday 17th April.
11am - 4.30pm (last admission 4pm).

Admission Rates: Adults £3.50, Child £2.00 (under 5s free).

Groups Rates: Group Rates on application/subject to negotiation and discussion of exact requirements e.g. whether guide required, refreshments etc.

Facilities: Refreshments on sale from ticket office (cold drinks, confectionery)

Disabled Access: Yes. Parking for disabled on site.

Tours/Events: Tours by arrangement.

Coach Parking: Yes

Length of Visit: Allow 1 1/2 - 2 Hours

Booking Contact: Jack Doyle
Westonbirt School, Tetbury, Gloucestershire, GL8 8QG
Telephone: 01666 881338 Fax: 01666 880364

Email: doyle@westonbirt.gloucs.sch.uk

Website: www.westonbirt.gloucs.sch.uk

Location: On A433, 3 miles SW of Tetbury, opposite Westonbirt Arboretum which is clearly marked by brown tourist information signs form all directions.

Please quote this guide when booking

Westonbirt, The National Arboretum   Gloucestershire

Westonbirt is a wonderful world of trees and is beautiful at any time of year. Set in 600 acres of glorious Cotswold countryside, it has 17 miles of paths along which to stroll and over 18,000 numbered trees, including 100 champions - the oldest, largest, tallest of that species in the country.

In spring it is ablaze with colour from rhododendrons, azaleas, magnolias and bluebells, but is more famous for its autumn colour, when it seems almost every tree turns a brilliant red, orange or gold. Summer brings cool leafy glades where butterflies and bees busily collect nectar, and an exciting events programme including The Festival of Wood. Add to this a restaurant, shop and plant centre and you have a perfect day out.

Fact File

Opening Times:	10am - 8pm or dusk if earlier.
Admission Rates:	Adults from £5.00 - £7.50 subject to seasonal variation. £1.00 for Children 5-18yrs Concessions and family tickets available. Please see website for confirmation at time of visit.
Group Rates:	Group rates available, please telephone for details.
Facilities:	Shop, Plant Sales, Cafe, Restaurant.
Disabled Access:	Yes. Toilet and parking for disabled on site. Wheelchairs on loan, booking necessary.
Tours/Events:	Festival of Wood - August, Enchanted Wood - December, Summer Concerts
Coach Parking:	Yes
Length of Visit:	2 - 3 hours
Booking Contact:	Helen Daniels Westonbirt Arboretum, Tetbury, Gloucestershire, GL8 8QS. Telephone: 01666 880220 Fax: 01666 880559
Email:	westonbirt@forestry.gsi.gov.uk
Website:	www.forestry.gov.uk/westonbirt
Location:	15 mins north east of Junction 18 M4.

Please quote this guide when booking

Trull House Garden   Gloucestershire

The gardens were laid out in the early 20th Century and this structure has been added to since then. The principle features are the lily pond, the sunken garden, the wilderness and the walled gardens.

Within the walled gardens behind the house are herbaceous borders that contain many unusual plants cleverly planted providing a spectacle from May to September. In front of the beautiful Cotswold Stone House are large expanses of lawn surrounded by mature trees. Views from the gardens are breathtaking.

The cosy atmosphere and size of the garden (8 acres) make it an ideal place to visit whether individually or as a group. Home made teas are available and other refreshments can be arranged for groups. Access and parking are easy.

The garden was featured in Country Living and Roots and Shoots in 2003. A haven in the Cotswolds not to be missed.

Fact File

Opening Times:	Wednesdays, Saturdays and Bank Holidays- 29th April - 30th August 2006. Most Sundays - Please telephone to confirm.
Admission Rates:	Adults £3.50, Children under 16 free.
Group Rates:	Minimum group size: 20+ Adults £3.50, Children under 16 free. Free guided tour included
Facilities:	WC, Plant Sales, Pots and Garden Furniture for sale.
Disabled Access:	Yes.
Tours/Events:	Please call for details.
Coach Parking:	Yes
Length of Visit:	1 + hours
Booking Contact:	Simon Mitchell Trull House, Nr. Tetbury, Gloucestershire, GL8 8SQ. Telephone: 01285 841255
Email:	simonmitchell@btconnect.com
Website:	www.trullhouse.co.uk
Location:	3 miles east of Tetbury off A433. Follow signs.

Please quote this guide when booking

Exbury Gardens & Steam Railway — Hampshire

Natural beauty is in abundance at Exbury Gardens, a 200 - acre woodland garden on the east bank of the Beaulieu River. Created by Lionel de Rothschild in the 1920's the Gardens are a stunning vision of his inspiration. The spring displays of rhododendrons, azaleas, camellias and magnolias are world famous. The daffodil meadow, rock garden, exotic garden and herbaceous and grasses garden, ponds and cascades ensure year round interest. Exbury is a previous winner of Christie's Garden of the Year.

The Exbury Gardens Railway proves very popular with visitors. Why not 'let the train take the strain' on a 1 1/4 mile journey over a bridge, through a tunnel, across a pond in the Summer Lane Garden planted with bulbs, herbaceous perennials and grasses? Then travel along the top of the rock garden and across a viaduct into the American Garden.

Groups booking a visit to see Exbury at its peak in April and May receive free tickets for a return visit in October /November, when the Autumn colours are spectacular.

Fact File

Opening Times: 1st March - 5th November 2006 10am - 5.30pm (High season 20 March - 4 June)

Admission Rates: (H/S-L/S) Adult £7.50/£5.00, Senior Citizen £7.00/£4.50, Child (3-15) £1.50/£1.00 under 3's Free, Family £17.50/£12.00, (2 Adults & 3 Children 3-15). Railway £3.00/£2.50 extra. See above for details of free return visit scheme.

Groups Rates: Minimum group size: 15 - Adults £7.00/£4.50.

Facilities: Gift Shop, Plant Sales, Teas, Restaurant, Buggy Tours.

Disabled Access: Yes. Toilet and parking for disabled on site. Wheelchairs on loan. Accessible carriages on train.

Tours/Events: Please call for info on guided tours & 'Meet & Greets' by arrangement on 023 80 891203. Please call for details of special events, or visit our website.

Coach Parking: Yes

Length of Visit: 2 - 3 hours, but up to 4 - 5 hours during main flowering season.

Booking Contact: Reception
Exbury Gardens, Estate Office, Exbury, Southampton, Hants SO45 1AZ.
Telephone: 023 80 891203 Fax: 023 80 899940

Email: nigel.philpott@exbury.co.uk

Website: www.exbury.co.uk

Location: Junction 2 west of M27, just follow A326 to Fawley, off B3054, 3 miles Beaulieu. Signposted.

Please quote this guide when booking

Mottisfont boasts thirty acres of landscaped grounds with sweeping lawns and magnificent trees, set amidst glorious countryside along the River Test.

The extensive gardens were remodelled gradually during the 20th century. Norah Lindsay designed a parterre, Geofrey Jellicoe redesigned the north front with an avenue of pollarded limes and an octagon of yews, all combine to provide interest throughout the seasons. Graham Stuart Thomas designed the walled garden in 1972, with beds divided by attractive box hedges, to contain the NATIONAL COLLECTION of OLD FASHIONED ROSES, with over 300 varieties. It is at its best in mid June, but has plenty to interest visitors later in summer and autumn.

The twelfth century Augustine priory is now a house of some note, containing delightful rooms such as the drawing room decorated by Rex Whistler in "trompe l'oeil" fantasy style. It also houses an interesting collection of 19th and early 20th century pictures donated by painter Derek Hill.

Fact File

Opening Times:	Please telephone the information line for details 01794 341220.
Admission Rates:	Adults £7.00, Senior Citizen £7.00, Child, £3.50, Family £17.50
Group Rates:	Minimum group size: 15
	Group rate £6.00 per adult.
Facilities:	Visitor Centre, Shop, Plant Sales, Teas, Kitchen Cafe.
Disabled Access:	Yes. Toilet and Parking for disabled on site. Wheelchairs on loan.
Tours/Events:	See Mottisfont event brochure.
Coach Parking:	Yes
Length of Visit:	2 hours
Booking Contact	Liz Dean. Mottisfont Abbey, Mottisfont, Nr Romsey, Hampshire, SO51 0LP
	Telephone 01794 340757 Fax: 01794 341492
Email:	mottisfontabbey@nationaltrust.org
Website:	www.nationaltrust,org
Location:	Signposted off A3057, Romsey to Stockbridge road, 4 miles north of Romsey.

Please quote this guide when booking

Sir Harold Hillier Gardens   Hampshire

Sir Harold Hillier Gardens is one of the most important modern plant collections in the world. Established in 1953 by the distinguished plantsman Sir Harold Hillier, the magnificent collection of over 42,000 plants from temperate regions around the world grows in a variety of superb themed landscaped set over 180-acres of rolling Hampshire countryside.

Open throughout the year, every part of the Gardens offers beauty, inspiration and discovery whatever the season and includes 11 National Plant Collections, over 250 Champion Trees and the largest winter Garden in Europe.

A £3.5 million Visitor & Education Pavilion offers fine views of the collection and surrounding countryside and features; a stylish licensed restaurant for home-cooked meals; light refreshments and afternoon teas; open-air terrace; gift shop; and interpretation area explaining the role and history of the Gardens. Entry to the Pavilion is free of charge with Group bookings welcome by prior arrangement.

Fact File

Opening Times:	Daily: 10.30am - 6pm or dusk if earlier. Open all year except Christmas Day and Boxing Day.
Admission Rates:	(From 01/04/06) Adults £7.75, Concession £6.50, Senior Citizen £6.50, Child under 16 yrs free.
Groups Rates:	Minimum group size 10. Adults £6.00, Senior Citizen £6.00.
Facilities:	£3.5 million Visitor & Education Pavilion, Open-air terrace and restaurant, Gift Shop, Plant Centre.
Disabled Access:	Yes. Toilet and parking for disabled on site. Wheelchairs on loan, booking advised, Mobility Scooters for hire.
Tours/Events:	Pre-booked guided tour with Curator, Botanist, Head Gardener and Horticultural staff available by arrangement. Please telephone for details about Special Events.
Coach Parking:	Yes (Free)
Length of Visit:	2 - 4 hours
Booking Contact:	Group Bookings. Sir Harold Hillier Gardens, Jermyns Lane, Romsey, Hampshire, SO51 0QA Telephone: 01794 369317/318 Fax: 01794 368027
Email:	info@hilliergardens.org.uk **Website:** www.hilliergardens.org.uk
Location.	The Gardens are situated, 3 miles north-east of Romsey. M3/M27 (West) to Romsey town centre. At Romsey follow brown heritage signs to the Hillier Gardens off the A3090. Alternatively, the Gardens can be approached from the A3057 Andover direction.

Please quote this guide when booking

Staunton Country Park   Hampshire

The Garden and landscape of Sir George Staunton, nineteenth century traveller and horticulturalist.

This Grade 2 listed site includes restored 1845 tropical glasshouses with rainforest flora, as well as the magnificent 1852 tropical lily house where the giant Amazon lily and tropical fish can be encountered.

Explore the Walled Garden with its crinkle-crankle wall and trained fruit trees, herbs, vegetables and colourful seasonal interest.

Discover the Queen's Golden Jubilee Maze and puzzle garden. Relax amongst fine specimen trees and the sensory garden.

There is also the Regency Oval Garden, leading to the ornamental farm where you can meet and feed the animals.

Not to forget the Green Flag Award winning landscaped parkland, with semi-natural ancient woodland and ornamental lake. These 1,000 acres also boast follies including the Chinese Bridge, Shell House and 1830s Rotunda. The restored Victorian Coach House is also open for refreshments at weekends. (Weather permitting)

Fact File

Opening Times: 10 a.m. – 5 p.m. (closes 4 p.m. winter). Open all year (closed only Christmas Day).

Admission Rates: Adults: £4.60, Senior Citizens: £4.00, Children: £3.50 (Rates valid until March 2006)

Group Rates: Minimum Groups Size: 10
Adults: £3.70, Senior Citizens: £3.20, Children: £2.80 (Rates valid until March 2006)

Facilities: Visitor centre, shop plant sales, restaurant, teas, meetings and conference facilities, venue hire for private events.

Disabled Access: Yes. Toilet and car parking on site. Wheelchair Loan booking available.

Tours/Events: Guided tours available. Programme of guided walks thought the year.

Coach Parking: Yes

Length of Visit: 2 – 4 hours

Booking Contact   Chris Bailey. Staunton Country Park, Middle Parkway, Havant, Hampshire PO9 5HB
Telephone: 023 9245 3405 Fax: 023 9249 8156

Email: Staunton.park@hants.gov.uk

Website: www.hants.gov.uk/staunton

Location: J12, M27, just off A27 (to Havant). Off B2149 Petersfield Road, follow brown signs between Havant and Horndean.

Please quote this guide when booking

West Green House Gardens   Hampshire

Nestling in a woodland corner of Hampshire is this ravishingly attractive 1720's manor house, where busts of gods, emperors and dukes look down from the walls onto two major gardens. The inner gardens, enclosed by eighteenth century walls, are all devoted to parterres. One is filled with water lilies, another of classical design with box topiary and a third enacts the whimsy of *Alice in Wonderland* with the story's characters in ivy and box topiary surrounded by roses of red and white. The main walled garden is planted in subtle hues of mauve, plum and blue, contained in beds that have been faithfully restored to their original outlines. A decorative potager is centred around berry-filled fruit cages where herbs, flowers and unusual vegetables are designed into colourful patterns. All this is surrounded by a second garden, a remarkable new-classical park studded with follies, birdcages and monuments. In 2004 a Paradise water garden was opened.

West Green House was the first garden to have a whole `Gardeners World' programme dedicated to itself.

Fact File

Opening Times:	Open 14th April to 30th September, Wednesday thru to Sunday 11am - 4.30pm
	Garden Shop open October to 23rd December 11am - 4pm (Free).
Admission Rates:	April to September Adults £5.00, Children £2.50.
Group Rates:	Groups by arangement please telephone for details.
Facilities:	Tea Rooms, Nursery, Garden Shop.
Disabled Access:	Yes. Toilet and parking for disabled on site.
Tours/Events:	Easter Saturday Plant Fair, Easter Sunday Easter Egg & Summer Bulb Hunt.
	Midsummer Mediterranean Fair 18th June. Opera 29th & 30th July. 5th & 6th August.
Coach Parking:	Yes
Length of Visit:	2 hours approximately.
Booking Contact:	West Green House, Thackhams Lane, West Green, Hartley Wintney, Hants RG27 8JB
	Telephone: 01252 845582 Fax: 01252 844611
Email:	None
Website:	westgreenhousegardens.co.uk
Location:	10 miles north east of Basingstoke, 1 mile west of Hartley Wintney, 1 mile north of A30.

Please quote this guide when booking

Hergest Croft Gardens   Herefordshire

From Spring bulbs to Autumn colour, this is a garden for all seasons. With over 60 champion trees, the Gardens are recognised as "one of the best collections of woody plants held in private ownership", holding National Collections of Maples, Birches and Zelkovas. Rhododendrons and Azaleas are spectacular in Spring, and the large kitchen garden with the long double herbaceous borders, Rose Garden and Spring Borders are always attractive. Autumn colours are superb.

Teas with local home-made food are available in the old dining-room. Rare and unusual plants are for sale, the majority grown in the garden, and there is a shop selling a wide range of gifts.

There are special entry rates for pre-booked groups of 20 or more people.

Fact File

Opening Times:	Weekends in March 12-30pm - 5.00pm.
	1st April to 29th October Daily. May to June 12.00pm - 6.00pm. All other 12.30pm - 5.30pm
Admission Rates:	Adults £5.00, Senior Citizen £5.00, Child Free
Group Rates:	Minimum group size: 20 +
	Adults £4.00, Senior Citizen £4.00, Child Free
Facilities:	Shop, Plant Sales, Light Lunches and Teas.
Disabled Access:	Yes. but limited to certain areas. Toilet and parking for disabled.
	Wheelchair on loan.
Tours/Events:	Pre booked guided tours @ £6.00 (including entrance) Monday 1st May Flower Fair,
	Sunday 15th October Autumn Plant Fair.
Coach Parking:	Yes
Length of Visit:	2 + Hours
Booking Contact:	Melanie Lloyd
	Hergest Croft Gardens, Kington, Herefordshire, HR5 3EG
	Telephone: 01544 230160 Fax: 01544 232031
Email:	gardens@hergest.co.uk
Website:	www.hergest.co.uk
Location:	Follow brown tourist signs off the A44 to Rhayader.

Please quote this guide when booking

Shipley Gardens Herefordshire

Horticultural Secretaries may wish to book their group into a mid-week or weekend visit to take in other gardens and attractions of Herefordshire. Bob Macadie of Shipley (01423 870356) talks to groups about the philosophy of his own gardens and would be pleased to put forward an optional itinerary based upon the adjacent Warners Herefordshire Holme Lacy Hotel.

Shipley is a plants person's gardens of tranquillity, humour and learning, with lecterns of whimsical information, within a Wye Valley setting of scenic splendour.

Set within 30 acres of mixed environmental habitats as a magical structure of garden rooms of surprise and informality where temperate climate wild plants intermix and jostle with cultivated varieties amid structures of rare and interesting ornamental trees and shrubs. The gardens are managed as a home for birds, insects, butterflies and small mammals.

Fact File

Opening Times: Every day from 10am – 6pm from end of March until November frosts.
Admission Rates: £3.00
Group Rates: Minimum Groups Size: 12 £2.50
Facilities: Tea rooms with plant sales and shop.
Disabled Access: Yes. Toilet and car parking on site.
Tours/Events: Guided tours available.
Coach Parking: Yes
Length of Visit: 2 hours
Booking Contact Bob Macadie, Shipley Gardens, Holme Lacy, Herefordshire HR2 6LS
Telephone: 01432 870356
Email: bobmacadie@shipleygardens.plus.com
Website: www.shipleygardens.plus.com
Location: Well-signed coach entrance in Holme Lacy village on the B4399, 5 miles south-east of Hereford.

Located in a peaceful area of the Welsh Marches close to the historic half-timbered village of Pembridge the two-acre gardens are laid out to frame the splendid views across meadows to the surrounding hills. Within the garden a huge collection of moisture loving plants surrounds the tangle of streams and ponds behind the old corn mill, and there is an unusual natural bog where plants grow with lush abundance.

Numerous bridges connect the different areas of the garden, and you can walk through a forest of giant gunnera and around an adjacent wild flower meadow. Unusual features include a castellated stone tower with a dovecote and gargoyles which spout water raised by an old iron water wheel.

The garden was featured on BBC Gardeners' World in September 2003 and in the Daily Telegraph in June 2005, and is listed in the Good Gardens Guide.

Photograph By Sarah Cuttle

Fact File

Opening Times: Daily 1st April – 30th September, 11 a.m. – 5 p.m.
Admission Rates: Adults/Senior Citizens: £3.50 Children: £1.00
Group Rates: Minimum Groups Size: 15
Adults/Senior Citizens: £3.00 Children: £1.00
Facilities: Plant Sales, Restaurant, Teas.
Disabled Access: Yes, to 80% of garden. Toilet and car parking on site.
Tours/Events: Guided tours available.
Coach Parking: Yes
Length of Visit: 1 - 1½ hours
Booking Contact Richard Pim, Westonbury Mill Water Gardens, Pembridge, Hereforshire HR6 9HZ
Telephone: 01544 388650 Fax: 01544 388650
Email: richard@pim99.freeserve.co.uk
Location: Between Leominster and Kington, sign posted from the A44 1½ miles west of Pembridge.

Please quote this guide when booking

The garden at Hatfield House dates from the early 17th century when Robert Cecil, 1st Earl of Salisbury, employed John Tradescant the Elder to plant and lay it out around his new home.

Tradescant was sent to Europe where he found and brought back trees, bulbs, plants and fruit trees, which had never previously been grown in England. This beautifully designed garden included orchards, elaborate fountains, scented plants, water parterres, terraces, herb gardens and a foot maze.

Following the fashion for landscape gardening and some neglect in the 18th century, restoration of the garden started in earnest in Victorian times. Lady Gwendoline Cecil, younger daughter of Prime Minister Salisbury, designed the West Garden as it is today. The East Garden was laid out by the 5th Marquess of Salisbury. The present Dowager Lady Salisbury dedicated 30 years to the restoration and improvement of the gardens that now bear her indelible imprint.

Today, the garden to the West of the house, which includes the Herb, Knot and Wilderness areas, can be seen throughout the open season.

Fact File

Opening Times:	Easter Saturday - end September, 11am - 5.30pm.
Admission Rates:	Adults £4.50, Senior Citizen £4.50, Child £3.50 (Thursday £7.00 - no concessions).
Facilities:	Tea Room, Restaurant, Gift Shop, Park Nature Trails.
Disabled Access:	Yes. Toilet and parking for disabled on site.
Tours/Events:	Flower Festival 10-11th June.
	Hatfield House Country Show 18th - 20th August
Coach Parking:	Yes
Length of Visit:	2 1/2 hours
Booking Contact:	The House Office
	Hatfield House, Hatfield, Hertfordshire. AL9 5NQ
	Telephone: 01707 287010 Fax: 01707 287033
Email:	visitors@hatfield-house.co.uk
Website:	www.hafield-house.co.uk
Location:	21 miles north of London. M25 junction 23, seven miles. A1(M) junction 4 two miles. Signed of A414 and A1000. Opposite Hatfield Rail Station.

Knebworth House Gardens and Park   Hertfordshire

The present 25-acre garden dates largely from the Victorian and Edwardian eras, with more recent, and continuing, restoration and additions. Sir Edwin Lutyens re-designed the formal gardens immediate to the House in the early 1900's.

Each of the 'rooms' within the garden has its own identity, colour and flowering time. The Sunken Lawn, the main features of which are the twin avenues and a central square of 'pollarded limes'. The Rose Garden with lily ponds and herbaceous borders provide a centrepiece to the garden. The Brick Garden with blue and silver plantings and a pergola. The wilderness and Woodland Walk which is a carpet of daffodils in spring followed by blue alkanet, foxgloves and other wild flowers now has the added attraction of a dinosaur trail. Other 'room's include the Green Garden; Gold Garden; Malus Walk; Pets' Cemetery; the Maze; the Walled Garden with culinary herbs and vegetables and the Jekyll Herb Garden designed by Gertrude Jekyll in 1907.

(Photograph shows the Rose Garden with the Sunken Lawn and Knebworth House in the background).

Fact File

Opening Times:	Daily 1 April - 17 April, 27 May - 4 June, 1 July - 5 Sept
	Weekends & Bank Holidays, 25-26 March, 22 April - 21 May, 10-25 June, 9-24 Sept
	Park, Playground & Gardens: 11.00 - 17.30. House 12.00 - 17.00
Admission Rates:	Adults £7.00, Seniors / children £7.00 (All excluding House).
	(Supplement to visit the House: Adults: £2.00, Seniors / children £1.50)
Group Rates:	Minimum group size: 20. Adults £6.00, Seniors / children £6.00 (All excluding House).
	(Supplement to visit the House: Adults: £2.00, Seniors / children £1.50)
Facilities:	Car & Coach Parking, Toilets, Shop, Garden Terrace Tea Room, Picnic Area.
Disabled Access:	Toilet and parking for disabled on site, A wheelchair is available for use.
Tours/Events:	Pre-booked guided garden tours available for groups of 20 plus
	20-21st May, Hertfordshire Garden Show.
Coach Parking:	Yes
Length of Visit:	3 hours
Booking Contact:	Knebworth House Gardens and Park, Knebworth, Hertfordshire. SG3 6PY
	Telephone: 01438 812661 Fax: 01438 811908
Email:	info@knebworthhouse.com
Website:	www.knebworthhouse.com
Location:	28 miles north of central London, direct access from Junction 7 of the A1M.

Please quote this guide when booking

Osborne House Garden   Isle of Wight

The terraces have been restored to their Victorian layout and are once again planted in seasonally changing Victorian bedding. The walled fruit and flower garden has been restored. Features include a variety of Victorian trained fruit trees, expansive cut flower borders and rose and fruit arches. Herbaceous borders are planted with sub tropical and unusual species, very fashionable at the time of Queen Victoria.

See pleasure grounds containing mature specimens of unusual trees, many of which were some of the first introductions into Britain. The garden adjoining the Swiss Cottage was built for Victoria and Albert's children to learn the domestic skills of gardening. Vegetables and fruit were grown which were sold to Price Albert, at commercial rates, providing the children with a practical exercise in market gardening.

The Ring Walk has been restored and takes in historic features like the mount, pond and the restored ice-house.

Fact File

Opening Times: 1st April - 3oth September, 10am - 6pm daily: October 10 - 4pm daily.
1st November -31st March limited opening, please contact site for details.

Admission Rates: House & Grounds, (Grounds) Adult £9.30 (£5.50) Senior Citizen £7.00 (£4.10), Child £4.70 (£2.80). Family £23.30 (£13.80).

Group Rates: Minimum group size: 11. 15% discount for groups of 11 persons or more when all tickets are purchased together.

Facilities: Gift Shop, Plant Sales, Teas, Restaurant, Baby Changing, Toilets,

Disabled Access: Partial. Toilet and parking for disabled on site. Wheelchair on loan.

Tours/Events: None

Coach Parking: Yes

Length of Visit: 3 hours

Booking Contact: Osborne House, York Avenue, East Cowes, Isle of Wight. PO32 6JY
Telephone: 01983 200022 Fax: 01983 281380

Email: None

Website: www.english-heritage.org.uk

Location: 1 mile south east of East Cowes (map190i ref 3Z510940).
Buses - Southern Vectis Services 4 Ryde - East Cowes and 5 Newport - East Cowes.

Please quote this guide when booking

There's magic and mystery, history and romance at this enchanting award-winning venue - which provides such an unusual combination of a traditional heritage garden with the contemporary landscaping of the ancient woodland.

First laid out in 1674 on a gentle, south-facing slope, the formal walled gardens are set against the romantic backdrop of a medieval moat house (not open to the public). They include herbaceous borders, an exquisite white rose garden with over 20 varieties of roses, a secret garden, knot garden, nut walk, paradise walk and oriental garden plus the drunken garden with its crazy topiary, and there's wonderful seasonal colour throught spring, summer and autumn.

In complete contrast, in the ancient woodland of the 'Enchanted Forest" there are quirky and mysterious gardens developed by innovative designer, Ivan Hicks.

Fact File

Opening Times:	1st April - 4th November, daily 10.00am - 5.30pm (or dusk if earlier).
Admission Rates:	Adults £8.70, Senior Citizen £7.20, Child (3-12yrs) £7.20, Family Ticket (2+2) £29.50.
Group Rates:	Minimum group size: 20
	Adults £7.25, Senior Citizens July - August £6.25 (off peak £5.50), Students £6.25, School/Youth Groups £5.50.
Facilities:	Gift Shop, Licensed Restaurant, Plant Sales.
Disabled Access:	Yes. Toilet & limited parking for disabled on site. Wheelchairs on loan.
Tours/Events:	Guided tours for groups - pre booked only, £30 per guide. Packed programme of Special Events throughout the season.
Coach Parking:	Yes
Length of Visit:	3 - 4 hours
Booking Contact:	Carrie Goodhew
	Groombridge Place, Groombridge, Tunbridge, Wells, Kent TN3 9QG
	Telephone 01892 861444 Fax: 01892 863996
Email:	office@groombridge.co.uk
Website:	www.groombridge.co.uk
Location:	4 miles south west of Tunbridge Wells on B2110, just off the A264 between Tunbridge Wells and East Grinstead.

Please quote this guide when booking

Hall Place & Gardens   Kent

Hall Place is a fine Tudor mansion built almost 500 years ago in the reign of Henry VIII for the Lord Mayor of London, Sir John Champneys. It boasts a magnificent panelled Tudor Great Hall and Minstrels Gallery, and views over award winning gardens, with topiary, herb garden, secret garden, Italianate garden, Flora-for-Fauna garden and inspirational herbaceous borders. In its former walled gardens is a plant nursery and sub-tropical plant house where you can see ripening bananas in mid-winter.

A recent addition is the Educational Environmental Garden (wheelchair access), divided into Tudor Garden (looking at plants used for dyeing, medicine, beauty and cooking), meadow land, bug hunt ground and dipping pond.

There is a shop and numerous exhibitions, including an opportunity to purchase artists' work. Various rooms, including the Great Hall are available for hire for weddings and other events.

Fact File

Opening Times: Gardens: All Year. House: 1st April - 31st October Mon - Sat (10 - 5), Bank Hol & Sun (11 - 5), 1st November - 31st March Tues - Sat (10 - 4.15), Closed Sun & Mon.

Admission Rates: Free Admission

Group Rates: There is a charge for pre-booked guided tours.

Facilities: Gift Shop, Plant Sales, Teas, Restaurant.

Disabled Access: Partial. Toilet and parking for disabled on site.

Tours/Events: Pre-booked guided tours available of House and/or garden. A year long programme of events.

Coach Parking: Yes

Length of Visit: 3 - 4 hours

Booking Contact: Mrs J Hearn-Gillham
Bourne Road, Bexley, Kent, DA5 1PQ
Telephone: 01322 526574 Fax: 01322 522921

Email: jhearn-gillham@btconnect.com

Website: www.hallplaceandgardens.com

Location: Black Prince Interchange of the A2, 3 miles from Junction 2 on the M25, towards London, Nearest rail connection Bexley. Buses 229, 492, B15,132 to the foot of Gravel Hill.

Please quote this guide when booking

Lullingstone Castle and World Garden   Kent

Winner of the UK's Best New Tourism Project Award in 2005. Set within 120 acres of beautiful Kent countryside, Lullingstone Castle is one of England's oldest family estates. The manor house and gatehouse – which overlook a stunning 15 acre lake – were built in 1497 and have been home to the same family ever since. In 2005, Tom Hart Dyke – 20th generation of Hart Dykes to live at Lullingstone – created within the Castle grounds a unique and inspiring 'World Garden' and filled it with thousands of rare, unusual and beautiful plants collected from all over the world (Tom came up with the idea for the garden whilst being held hostage at gunpoint in the Colombian jungle in 2000!) By the 2006 season these plants will have established and begun to fill the borders – which are designed in the shape of the continents.

Tom would now like to offer your group a chance to join him on a unique and personal tour of the 'World Garden'. You will also have the opportunity to view inside his home – Lullingstone Castle.

Fact File

Opening Times: 1st April to 30th October. Fridays and Saturdays 12pm - 5pm, Sundays 2pm - 6pm. Pre-booked groups are also welcomed on Wednesdays and Thursdays.

Admission Rates: House & Grounds Adults £5.50, Senior Citizen £5.00, Child £2.50, Family £12.50.

Group Rates: Minimum group size: 15
Adults £4.50 per person plus £35.00 per group for Tom or a dedicated guide.

Facilities: Toilets, book and plant sales on site. Visitor Centre and cafe 400m easy stroll alongside River Darent.

Disabled Access: Yes. Toilet and parking for disabled on site.

Tours/Events: A Special group tour with Tom Hart Dyke may be booked in advance.
Plant Fairs – ring for details.

Coach Parking: Yes.

Length of Visit: Guided tour of House and Garden lasts approximately 2 - 2 1/2 hours.

Booking Contact: Mr and Mrs G Hart Dyke
Lullingstone Castle, Eynsford, Kent DA4 0JA.
Tel: 01322 862114 Fax: 01322 862115

Email: mail@publicity-works.org

Website: www.lullingstonecastle.co.uk

Location: Off the A225 near the village of Eynsford and just 10 minutes drive from Junction 3 of M25.

Please quote this guide when booking

Penshurst Place & Gardens

Kent

Ancestral home of the Sidney family since 1552, with a history going back six and half centuries, Penshurst Place has been described as "the grandest and most perfectly preserved example of a fortified manor house in all England".

See the awe-inspiring Barons Hall with its 60ft high steeply angled roof and the State Rooms filled with fine tapestries, furniture, portraits and armour. The 11 acres of Gardens are as old as the original house - the walls and terraces were added in the Elizabethan era - and are divided into a series of self-contained garden rooms. Each garden room offers an abundance of variety in form, foliage and bloom and ensures a continuous display from Spring to Autumn.

There is also a Park with Woodland Trail, a Garden History Exhibition, a Toy Museum, Venture Playground, Shop, and Garden Tea Room, which contribute to a great day out.

Fact File

Opening Times:	Weekends from the 4th March, Daily from 25th March - 29th October.
Admission Rates:	**House & Gardens:** Adults £7.50, Senior Citizen £7.00, Child £5.00.
Groups Rates:	Minimum group size: 20
	Including garden tour: Adults £8.50, Senior Citizen £8.50, Child £4.50
Facilities:	Shop, Teas & Garden History Exhibition in Garden Tower.
Disabled Access:	Yes. Toilet and parking for disabled on site, Wheelchairs on loan, booking necessary.
Tours/Events:	Garden tours available for pre-booked groups.
	NB Special "Garden Tours & Cream Tea" offer for groups.
Coach Parking:	Yes.
Length of Visit:	2 - 3 hours
Booking Contact:	Caroline Simpson
	Penshurst Place, Penshurst, Kent TN11 8DG
	Telephone: 01892 870307 Fax: 01892 870866
Email:	enquiries@penshurstplace.com
Website:	www.penshurstplace.com
Location:	M25 junction 5, follow A21 to Hastings. Exit at Hildenborough then follow brown tourists signs.

Please quote this guide when booking

Scotney Castle   Kent

A hidden gem waiting to be discovered Scotney lies nestled in the valley of the river Bewl. This fairy tale moated castle and its surrounding landscape compose an ideally romantic picture. Created in the 1830's by Edward Hussey III the result represents one of the last and most successful expressions of the picturesque movement. The plunging site, mixture of sheltered tranquil quarry and open lawn and the ragged silhouette of the old castle provide drama and beauty in abundance.

From early in the year snowdrops, primroses and daffodils cover the lawns surrounding the moat, whilst sweet smelling bluebells line the drive. Late spring brings magnificent displays of rhododendrons, azaleas and Kalmia Latifolia. As summer progresses white wisteria rambles across the ruined castle walls and the season reaches its dramatic finale with the sumptuous red's and gold's of autumn provided by the superb liquid ambars and Japanese maples.

Fact File

Opening Times: Garden & Shop - 18th March - 29th October 2006. Old Castle - 29th April - 1st October.
Weds - Sun 11am - 6pm Last entry at 5pm or closing at dusk.
Open Bank Holiday Monday, Closed Good Friday.

Admission Rates: Adults £5.20, Senior Citizens £5.20, Children £2.60

Groups Rates: Minimum group size 15. Adults £4.80, Senior Citizens £4.80, Children £2.40

Facilities: Visitor Centre, Shop, Plant Sales.

Disabled Access: Yes. Partial due to steep slopes, map provided. Toilet and car parking on site.
Wheel chair available.

Tours/Events: Tours available at an extra charge please pre - book. Easter Trail, Halloween Spook & extra events, such as lectures, walks etc. throughout the year.

Coach Parking: Yes

Length of Visit: 1 1/2 - 2 Hours

Booking Contact: Miss K M Darvill, Scotney Castle, Lamberhurst, Kent, TN3 8JN
Telephone: 01892 891081 Fax: 01892 890110

Email: scotneycastle@nationaltrust.org.uk

Website: www.nationaltrust.org.uk/scotneycastle

Location: One mile south of Lamberhurst on the A21. Bus - Coastal Coaches 256.
Station - Wadhurst 5 1/2 miles away. Free parking on site

Please quote this guide when booking

Sissinghurst Castle Garden   Kent

Sissinghurst is a place that breathes old England, and yet the ideas behind its design, a series of intimate moments that together form a striking narrative - are very modern. Its Lime Walk, Herb Garden, Cottage Garden and above all the famous White Garden put on a kind of theatrical performance that marks the changing moods and colours of the seasons.

Vita Sackville-West and Harold Nicolson were an unusual couple - he a diplomat turned reviewer, she a writer and newspaper columnist who liked to work in a tower, not of ivory, but of warm pink brick.

Sissinghurst was originally built in the 1560's: once a poorhouse, and a prison, its Great Court was a ruin by the time the couple took it on in the 1930's. They built on the ancient template of a lost Elizabethan house to create a a bold new story: the result is a triumphant essay in English Style.

Fact File

Opening Times:	18th March to 29th October, Mondays, Tuesdays & Fridays 11am to 6.30pm. Saturdays, Sunday & Bank Holidays 10am to 6.30pm. Closed Wednesdays & Thursday.
Admission Rates:	Adults £7.80, Family (2 adults 3 children) £20.00, Child £3.50, national Trust Members Free
Group Rates:	Minimum group size: 11 - Please telephone for details. Booking necessary
Facilities:	Shop, Self Service Restaurant, Exhibition, Picnic Areas, Woodland Walks.
Disabled Access:	Yes. Toilet and Parking for disabled on site. Wheelchairs on loan.
Tours/Events:	None.
Coach Parking:	Yes.
Length of Visit:	2 1/2 hours
Booking Contact:	Samantha Snaith Sissinghurst Castle, Cranbrook, Kent, TN17 2AB Telephone: 01580 710700 Fax: 01580 710702
Email:	sissinghurst@nationaltrust.org.uk
Website:	www.nationaltrust.org.uk/sissinghurst
Location:	2 miles north east of Cranbrook, 1 mile east of Sissinghurst village (A262)

Please quote this guide when booking

Squerryes Court Manor House & Gardens   Kent

The garden surrounding Squerryes Court is beautiful througout the seasons. In 1700 the garden was laid out in the formal style. When the Warde family acquired Squerryes in 1731, they swept away most of the formal garden and relandscaped it in the natural style then fashionable. The bones of the old garden survived.

Following the storm of 1987, the Warde family restored some of the formal garden using the 1719 print as a guideline. Hedges, pleached limes and a hornbeam avenue were planted. Box edged parterres containing lavender, santolina and purple sage were laid out. The Edwardian herbaceous borders were replanted. In other areas of the garden new borders have been created. The Victorian rockery features some fine topiary. The restoration is ongoing in the woodland garden, The lake, spring bulbs, rhododendrons and azaleas make this garden interesting all year. The manor house is also open.

Fact File

Opening Times: 2nd April - 28th September, Wednesday, Thursday, Sunday & Bank Holiday Mondays. Garden open 11.30am, House open 1.00pm, last entry 4.30pm closes 5.00pm.

Admission Rates: House & Grounds, Adults £6.00, Senior Citizen £5.50, Child (under 16) £3.00. Family £13.50 Grounds only, Adults £4.00, Senior Citizen £3.50, Child (under 16) £2.00, Family £7.50

Group Rates: Pre-booked groups of 20+ welcome any day except Saturday, please telephone for details.

Facilities: Kiosk, Small Shop, Conservatory Tea Room open 11.30am for light lunches.

Disabled Access: Partial, please telephone for details. Toilet and parking for disabled on site.

Tours/Events: Please telephone for details.

Coach Parking: Yes.

Length of Visit: 2 hours

Booking Contact: Mrs Warde/Mrs White
Squerryes Court Manor House, Westerham, Kent, TN16 1SJ.
Telephone: 01959 562345 Fax: 01959 565949

Email: squerryes.court@squerryes.co.uk

Website: www.squerryes.co.uk

Location: 25 miles from London sign posted from A25. Half a mile west of centre of Westerham, ten minutes from exit 6 or 5 on the M25.

Please quote this guide when booking

Stoneacre

The gardens at Stoneacre surround a fine example of a medieval house. The house was restored and enlarged by Aymer Vallance in the 1920s. As there is no historic garden plan the tenants at Stoneacre are required to ensure the garden is appropriate and sympathetic to the house.

The current tenants have made considerable changes to the planting and the atmosphere of the garden. Coming from a fashion background their interest is in shape, texture and subtle colouring. The tenants are particularly keen to maintain the atmosphere and intimacy of a private residence.

The garden develops through the seasons with a variety of unusual plants and combinations. There is a selection of grasses that give delicacy and movement to the borders. Late summer culminates in a good show of perennial sunflowers, Echinaceas, Heleniums and seed heads.

The garden has been featured recently in House and Garden, The Daily Telegraph, Gardens Illustrated.

Fact File

Opening Times:	18th March – 11th October: 2 – 6 p.m. (last entry 5 p.m.): Wednesday and Saturday and Bank Holiday Mondays.
Admission Rates:	Adults: £2.60 (NT members free), Children: £1.30.
Group Rates:	Private groups at other times by arrangement. Please telephone for details.
Facilities:	Plant Sales.
Disabled Access:	Yes, partial. Toilet and car parking on site.
Tours/Events:	Guided tours available, must be pre-booked. NGS opening 11 June 11 – 6 p.m.
Coach Parking:	Yes – small/medium coaches.
Length of Visit:	1 - 1 1/2 hours.
Booking Contact	Mr. Graham Fraser Stoneacre, Otham, Kent ME15 8RS. Telephone: 01622 862871 Fax: 01622 862157
Email:	stoneacreNT@aol.com
Location:	4 miles SE of Maidstone from A20 or A274. Follow signs for Otham/Stoneacre.

Please quote this guide when booking

Yalding Organic Gardens Kent

Described in the Daily Telegraph as 'among the most inspirational garden acres anywhere, for everyone', the gardens are rapidly gaining a reputation for being amongst the very best in the South East. Nestling against a traditional backdrop of hop gardens and oast houses, the gardens trace garden history through sixteen landscaped displays, including a 13th century apothecary's garden, a Tudor Knot, a cottager's garden in the early 19th century and a stunning herbaceous border, inspired by Gertrude Jekyll. Yalding is run by HDRA, Britain's leading organic gardening organisation, so naturally the gardens also demonstrate the best ways of making compost and how to control pests and diseases without using pesticides.

Kids will love the Children's garden. Home cooking is a speciality, using vegetables and salads fresh from the garden whenever possible - delicious! The gardens regularly appear on TV, most recently in Grassroots and the Flying Gardener.

Fact File

Opening Times: 10am - 5pm Wednesday to Sunday. April to October. Also open on Bank Holiday.

Admission Rates: Adults £4.00, Concessions £3.50, Child £1.00.

Group Rates: Minimum group size: 14
Adults £3.00, Child £1.00.

Facilities: Visitor Centre, Shop, Plant sales, Teas, Restaurant.

Disabled Access: Yes. Toilet and parking for disabled on site.

Tours/Events: Monthly programme of events.

Coach Parking: Yes

Length of Visit: 2 hours

Booking Contact: Events Office
Yalding Organic Gardens, Benover Road, Yalding, Nr Maidstone, Kent, ME18 6EX
Telephone: 01622 814650 Fax: 01622 814650

Email: enquiry@gardenorganic.org.uk

Website: www.gardenorganic.org.uk

Location: Half a mile south of Yalding on the B2162, 6 miles south west of Maidstone.

Please quote this guide when booking

Williamson Park

Situated in a commanding position over looking the city of Lancaster, Willamson Park has a variety of formal and woodland walks through its 54 acre grounds.

The original parkland has many specimen trees planted amongst the dramatic rock formations, a legacy from the park's history as a stone quarry. In 2006 the arboretum walk will open which follows an interesting path through attractive specimen trees, including Liriodendron tulipflera, Metasequoia glyptostrboides and Crinodendron hookerianum. Many of the trees were planted in the later part of the 19th century, however the park has recently planted many new specimen trees to complement the landscape.

The park centre piece, the Ashton Memorial, is a magnificent folly built by Lord Ashton in 1907. The building offers magnificent views over the surrounding coast and countryside, The park also has a Tropical Butterfly House and small zoo. All the facilities are open daily except Christmas, Boxing and New Years Day. Please telephone for details. The park grounds are open throughout the year.

Fact File

Opening Times:	All Year
Admission Rates:	To Gardens Free. Adults £4.25, Senior Citizens £3.75, Child £2.75.
Groups Rates:	Minimum group size 10
	10% Discount
Facilities:	Gift Shop, Teas, Cafe, Historic Folly.
Disabled Access:	Partial. Toilets and parking for disabled on site.
Tours/Events:	Pre booked groups for the Butterfly House only.
	Please telephone for list of events or check our website www.williamsonpark.com
Coach Parking:	Yes
Length of Visit:	2 Hours
Booking Contact:	Elaine Charlton
	Williamson Park, Lancaster, LA1 1UX
	Telephone: 01524 33318 Fax: 01524 848338
Email:	office@williamsonpark.com
Website:	www.williamsonpark.com
Location:	From junction 33 or 34 follow signs for Lancaster brown tourism signs from then on.

Please quote this guide when booking

Rockingham Castle stands on the edge of an escarpment giving dramatic views over five counties and the Welland Valley below.

The Castle architecture has examples from every period of its 950 year history. Surrounding the castle some 12 acres of gardens largely following the foot print of the medieval castle which houses the vast 400 year old "Elephant Hedge" that divides the formal 17th century terraced garden. The circular Yew hedge stands on the site of the mot and bailey that provides a backdrop for the Rose garden. Below the castle is the stunning 19th century "Wild Garden" that was replanted with advice from Kew Gardens. There are some 200 different species including a remarkabe AILANTHUS altissima "Tree of Heaven" some fine SEQUOIA and a good DAVIDIA "Handkerchief Tree".

There is something to see in the garden throughout the year.

Fact File

Opening Times: Open 12noon - 5pm. Grounds open at 12 noon. Castle opens from 1pm. Easter (16th April) to the end of May on Sundays & Bank Holiday Mondays, June to September on Tuesdays, Sundays, Bank Holiday Mondays.

Admission Rates: House & Gardens: Adults £7.50, Senior Citizen £6.50, Child (5 - 16) £4.50, Family(2+2) £19.50 Grounds (Gardens, Salvin's Tower, Gift Shop & Licensed Tea Room) Adult & Child £4.50 (Not available when special events are held in the grounds).

Group Rates: Minimum group size:20 £6.50. Full information pack is available on request.

Facilities: Gift Shop, Restaurant, Audio Tour

Disabled Access: Yes. Toilet and Parking for disabled on site.

Tours/Events: Tours of garden with Head Gardener, Richard Stribley. For regular events see website.

Coach Parking: Yes.

Length of Visit: 2 1/2 - 3 hours

Booking Contact: Nicola Moss
Rockingham Castle, Rockingham, Market Harborough, Leicestershire, LE16 8TH
Telephone: 01536 770240 Fax: 01536 771692

Email: estateoffice@rockinghamcastle.com

Website: www.rockinghamcastle.com

Location: 1 mile north of Corby on A6003.

Please quote this guide when booking

Wartnaby Gardens Leicestershire

A traditional country house garden, with inner gardens sheltered with yew hedges. They contain a Rose Garden with a good collection of old and new Roses, a White Garden, Herbaceous Borders and a Purple Border.

The central garden leads to spring and woodland gardens around a series of ponds, planted with trillium, arisaema, primulas and a multitude of spring bulbs and ferns, Beyond, a new arboretum and woodland walk.

The main Arboretum has an interesting collection of trees and shrubs and leads from the Clock House to the end of the front drive on the north side. A well designed Vegetable Garden and Orchard leads from the Main Garden through a Hornbeam tunnel with Hellebores, Hostas and Allium; Geometric border patterns for vegetables and arches of Roses and Clematis. The Orchard centre has a large Arbour planted with red Vines and red climbing Roses.

Fact File

Opening Times: Sunday 26th February 2006 - "Promise of Spring" 11am - 3pm.
NGS Openings: Sunday 30th April - Plant Sale 11am - 4pm,
Sunday 18th June - Plant Fair (20 Nurserymen) 11am - 4pm.
4th April to 25th July every Tuesdays 9.30 - 12.30pm (RHS members free on Tuesdays only).

Admission Rates: Adults £2.50, (£2.00 on Sun 26th Feb "Promise of Spring").

Facilities: Refreshments - lunch, tea etc, Plant Sales.

Disabled Access: Yes. Toilet and parking for disabled on site. Suitable for wheelchairs.

Tours/Events: None.

Coach Parking: Yes

Length of Visit: 1 - 2 1/2 hours

Booking Contact: Wartnaby House, Wartnaby, Melton Mowbray, Leicestershire LE14 3HY
Telephone: 01664 822549 Fax: 01664 822231

Email: None

Website: www.wartnabyplantlabels.co.uk

Location: 4 miles north west of Melton Mowbray. From A606 turn left through AB Kettleby 5 miles east of A46.

Please quote this guide when booking

Normanby Hall Country Park   North Lincolnshire

Set in 300 acres of woodland and pleasure grounds, the Victorian walled garden is a unique experience. The garden has been carefully restored to its late Victorian heyday and grows fruit, flowers and vegetables dating from 1901 or earlier. Trained fruit, vegetable beds and cut flower borders are complemented by a range of glasshouses including a peach case, vinery, display house and fernery.

The huge herbaceous borders in the Secret Garden boast a colourful selection of unusual plants, whilst the Sunken Garden near the Hall is planted in pastel shades. There is also a parterre and rose beds, A 400ft long bog garden has been created in the base of the old ha-ha and a Victorian woodland garden is under development.

Fact File

Opening Times:
Park open all year, 9am - dusk.
Walled Garden open 10.30 am - 5pm in summer, 10.30am - 4pm in winter.

Admission Rates:
Adults £4.20, Senior Citizen (over 60's) £3.80, Child £2.10. (2005 prices)
Season Ticket admits 2 Adults & Children all year for £15.00. (2005 prices)

Groups Rates:
Minimum group size: 15 Freedom visit Adults £3.50, Senior Citizen £3.15, Child £1.75.
Visit with tour: Adult £5.50, Senior Citizen £5.15, Child £2.75, (includes admission to all areas)

Facilities:
Visitor Centre, Shop, Tea Room, Restaurant, Plant Sales.
Regency Hall & Farm Museum also open 1pm - 4.30pm daily, from 1st April - 29th Sept.

Disabled Access:
Yes. Toilet and parking for disabled on site.
Wheelchairs & motorised scooters on loan, booking necessary.

Tours/Events:
Guided tours of Walled Garden & Hall available - approx 1 1/2 hours
Special gardening events throughout the year.

Coach Parking:
Yes

Length of Visit:
3 - 4 hours

Booking Contact:
Stuart Campbell. Normanby Hall Country Park, Normanby, Scunthorpe, DN15 9HU
Telephone : 01724 720588 Fax: 01724 721248

Email:
normanbyhall@northlincs.gov.uk **Website:** www.northlincs.gov.uk/normanby

Location:
4 miles north of Scunthorpe off the B1430

Please quote this guide when booking

The Museum of Garden History is situated in a restored church building, next door to Lambeth Palace, on the banks of the River Thames. A reproduction 17th century knot garden has been created on the site of the graveyard where the tomb of 17th century plant hunters, the John Tradescants, father and son, can be seen, next to the tomb of William Bligh of the 'Bounty'.

The garden was designed by the Marchioness of Salisbury in 1981, and is based on a tradtional, geometric design. It is filled with plants that were grown in Britain during the 17th century, including roses, bulbs, perenials, biennials and annuals. Surrounding the knot garden are ornamental borders also planted to the same period theme. These incorporate some fine trees such as medlar, mulberry, strawberry tree and false acacia. Topiarised myrtle, rosemary, holly and bay can be seen. The museum houses a permanent collection of historic garden tools, artefacts and curiosities.

Fact File

Opening Times:	Every day- 10.30am to 5pm.
	Closed Monday 19th Dec 2005 to Monday 2nd Jan 2006 inclusive
Admission Rates:	Suggested donation Adults: £3.00, Concessions £2.50.
Facilities:	Shop, Plant Sales, Teas/Light Refreshments, Garden.
Disabled Access:	Yes but restricted.
Tours/Events:	Guided tours can be booked.
	Seasonal Exhibitions.
Coach Parking:	No.
Length of Visit:	2 hours.
Booking Contact	Heather Tyas
	Museum of Garden History, Lambeth Palace Road, London, SE1 7LB
	Telephone: 020 7401 8865 / ext 21 Fax: 020 7401 8869
Email:	info@museumgardenhistory.org
Website:	www.museumgardenhistory.org
Location:	Next door to Lambeth Palace, London SE1.

Capel Manor Gardens

Middlesex

Capel Manor gardens and estate surround a Georgian Manor House and Victorian Stables. The gardens are broadly divided into five zones:

Historic landscape – includes a walled garden, magnolia border, holly walk, Italianate maze and seventeenth century gardens.

Model gardens – a range of domestic gardens including Sunflower Street (relocated from The Chelsea Flower Show), a new garden designed by Kim Wilde and gardens dedicated to the late Queen Mother and Princess of Wales.

Trials garden – experimental and thought-provoking gardens, sponsored by Gardening Which?

Theme gardens

Wilderness and woodland gardens – best in Spring for daffodils, bluebells and azaleas.

All of this together with animal stock including Clydesdale horses, make the gardens an excellent family day out. Visitors see behind the scenes of greater London's specialist college of Horticulture, Floristry, Garden Design, Animal Care, Arboriculture and Countryside studies.

Fact File

Opening Times:	10am - 6pm (last entry 4.30pm). open daily March - October. Please telephone to check times.
Admission Rates:	Adults £5.00, Senior Citizens £4.00, Child £2.00, Family Ticket £12.00.
Group Rates:	Minimum group size: 20 Adults £4.50, Senior Citizen £3.50, Child £1.50.
Facilities:	Visitor Centre, Shop, Plant Sales, Restaurant, Dogs allowed entry on lead.
Disabled Access:	Yes. Parking for disabled on site. Wheelchairs on loan, booking necessary.
Tours/Events:	Please telephone for details of tours and events programme.
Coach Parking:	Yes
Length of Visit:	2 - 3 hours
Booking Contact:	Julie Ryan Capel Manor Gardens, Bullsmoor Lane, Enfield, Middx, EN1 4RQ Telephone: 0208 366 4442 Fax: 01992 717544
Email:	julie.ryan@capel.ac.uk
Website:	www.capel.ac.uk
Location:	Near junction 25 of M25

Please quote this guide when booking

The Birmingham Botanical Gardens & Glasshouses   W Midlands

Opened in 1832, the Gardens are a 15 acre 'Oasis of Delight' with over 200 trees and the finest collection of plants in the Midlands. The Tropical House, full of rainforest vegetation, includes many economic plants and a 24ft lily pond. Palms, tree ferns and orchids are displayed in the Subtropical House. The Mediterranean House features citrus fruits and conservatory plants while the Arid House conveys a desert scene. There is colourful bedding on the Terrace plus Rhododendrons, Rose, Rock, Herb and Cottage Gardens, Trials Ground and Historic Gardens. The Gardens are notably home to the National Bonsai Collection.

Other attractions include a Children's Playground, Children's Discovery Garden, exotic birds in indoor and outdoor aviaries, an art gallery and Sculpture Trail. Bands play on summer Sunday afternoons and Bank Holidays.

Fact File

Opening Times:	Open daily from 9am(10am Sundays)
	Closing: April to September - 7pm, October to March - 5pm (or dusk).
Admission Rates:	Adults £6.10, Senior Citizen £3.60, Child £3.60
Groups Rates:	Minimum group size: 10
	Adults £5.00, Senior Citizen £3.20, Child £3.20
Facilities:	Shop, Tea Room, Plant Sales, Children's Discovery Garden, Sculpture Trail, Aviaries, Organic Garden.
Disabled Access:	Yes. Toilet and parking for disabled on site. Wheelchairs on loan, booking necessary.
Tours/Events:	Tours by appointment. Please telephone for details of Special Events programme.
Coach Parking:	Yes by appointment.
Length of Visit:	2 - 4 hours
Booking Contact:	Tony Cartwright
	The Birmingham Botanical Gardens, Westborne Road, Edgbaston, Birmingham, B15 3TR
	Telephone: 0121 454 1860 Fax: 0121 454 7835
Email:	admin@birminghambotanicalgardens.org.uk
Website:	www.birminghambotanicalgardens.org.uk
Location:	Access from M5 junction 3 and M6. follow the signs for Edgbaston then brown tourist signs to Botanical Gardens.

Please quote this guide when booking

David Austin Roses

Wolverhampton

A large rose garden covering nearly two acres (0.8HA) and containing over 700 different varieties, considered by many to be one of the best rose gardens in the world. The garden is divided into five different areas each with their own style and mix of roses. David Austin Roses are, of course, home to the English Roses and so these roses are planted exclusively in the Renaissance Garden as well as scattered around the garden. There is a particularly good collection of Old Roses and Climbers and Ramblers in the Long Garden and Wild Roses and their hydrids in the Species Garden. Other plants that associate well with roses are also found-clematis, climbing up roses in the Long Garden and hardy perennials with roses in the mixed borders of the long garden. This garden also contains Hybrid Teas, Floribundas and English Roses planted in formal beds. There is something of interest twelve months of the year with the early Species Flowering in March, through to the last flowers of the season on the repeat flowering roses braving the elements in November and December.

Fact File

Opening Times:	9am - 5pm (7 days a week) (Garden and Garden Shop)
	9.30am - 4.30pm Tea Room
Admission Rates:	Free entry
Groups Rates:	(Please contact for more details) (Mon - Fri)
Facilities:	Shop, Plant Sales, Teas and Light Lunches
Disabled Access:	Yes. Parking for disabled on site.
Tours/Events:	Workshops with the RHS and Guided Tours
Coach Parking:	Yes
Length of Visit:	2 - 3 Hours
Booking Contact:	Christobel Timmins
	David Austin Roses, Bowling Green Lane, Albrighton, Wolverhampton WV7 3HB.
	Telephone: 01902 376376 Fax: 01902 372142
Email:	plant_centre@davidaustinroses.co.uk
Website:	www.davidaustinroses.com
Location:	Albrighton is situated between the A41 and A464 about 8 miles west of Wolverhampton and 2 miles south east of junction 3 on the M54. Look for the brown tourist information signs.

Please quote this guide when booking

The UK's premier centre for organic gardening, now with - The Vegetable Kingdom - a family friendly, fully interactive visitor centre telling the story of Britain's vegetables and the importance of preserving rare varieties.

Outside there are ten acres of gardens, including stunning flower borders, herbs, shrubs, a delightful children's garden and, of course, lots of interesting and unusual vegetables and fruit .

Also, learn the best ways of making compost and how to control pests, diseases and weeds without using chemicals.

Enjoy a delicious home cooked meal in our restaurant, or relax with organic cappuccino in the garden cafe. A greatly enlarged new shop provides lots to tempt you!

Fact File

Opening Times:	9am - 5pm.
Admission Rates:	Adults £5.00, Senior Citizen £4.50, Child £2.50
Facilities:	Visitor Centre, Shop, Plant Sales, Teas, Restaurant.
Disabled Access:	Yes. Toilet and Parking for disabled on site. Wheelchairs on loan, booking necessary.
Tours/Events:	Regular programme of events, tours bookable.
Coach Parking:	Yes.
Length of Visit:	Half a day
Booking Contact:	Events Office. Ryton Organic Gardens, Coventry, CV8 3LG. Telephone: 02476 308211 Fax: 02476 639229
Email:	enquiry@hdra.org.uk
Website:	www.gardenorganic.org.uk
Location:	Off The A45 on the road to Wolston 5 miles south east of Coventry.

Please quote this guide when booking

Fairhaven Woodland & Water Garden   Norfolk

Fairhaven Woodland and Water Garden is a haven of peace and tranquillity in the heart of the Norfolk Broads.

Three miles of scenic paths. Environmentally managed for the thriving and varied wildlife. Delightful in Spring; primroses, daffodils, skunk cabbage (Lysichitum Americanum), bluebells, followed by a spectacular display of the largest naturalised collection of Candelabra primulas in England, and azaleas and rhododendrons. An oasis in Summer, with boat trips on our private broad, flowering shrubs and wild flowers which attract several species of butterflies. Glorious Autumn colours and quietly beautiful in Winter with wonderful reflections in the still water.

A full programme of special events is available including our Green/Environmental festival. Please ring for deails or visit our website.

Fact File

Opening Times: Open daily 10am - 5pm (dusk in winter) also open until 9pm on Wednesday and Thursday evenings from May to the end of August (Closed Christmas Day).

Admission Rates: Adult £4.00, Senior Citizen £3.50, Child £1.50 under 5's Free, Dogs 25p.
Annual Membership: Family £35.00, Single £15.00, Dogs £2.50.

Groups Rates: Minimum group size: 15
Adults £3.75, Senior Citizen £3.25, Child £1.25

Facilities: Visitor Centre, Gift Shop, Tea Room, Plant Sales, Boat trips April to end October.

Disabled Access: Yes. Toilet and parking for disabled on site. Wheelchairs on loan. Booking necessary.

Tours/Events: Guided walks or introductory talk for pre-booked groups. Programme of Special Events available, including guided walks, music in the Garden, Green/Environmental Festival and Halloweén event.

Coach Parking: Yes   **Length of Visit:** 2 - 3 hours or preferably all day.

Booking Contact: Mrs Beryl Debbage
Fairhaven Woodland & Water Garden, School Road, South Walsham, Norwich NR13 6DZ
Telephone/Fax: 01603 270449

Email: fairhavengardens@norfolkbroads.com

Website: www.norfolkbroads.com/fairhaven

Location: 9 miles east of Norwich, off B1140. Signposted on A47 at junction with B1140.

Please quote this guide when booking

Pensthorpe Nature Reserve and Gardens   Norfolk

Pensthorpe Nature Reserve is set in 500 acres of unspoilt Wensum Valley with miles of nature trails winding through ancient fen meadows and woodlands. A series of beautiful lakes is home to over 70 species of breeding birds, and dozens of migratory visitors pass through, including rare species like the Osprey and the Squacco Heron. A feature of Pensthorpe is its spectacular gardens, designed by Chelsea Flower Show award-winners Piet Oudolf and Julie Toll. Piet's naturalistic Millennium Garden is now fully established, with its deep borders of grasses and perennials planted in bold drifts creating dramatic waves of texture and colour. Visit at its spectacular best during June to September. Julie's new Wave Garden, planted early in 2005, will come into its own from Spring 2006. Its natural 'wild meadow' style incorporates small areas of seating overlooking the lakes, an ideal haven for peaceful contemplation.

Fact File

Opening Times: Jan - Mar 10am - 4pm; Apr - Dec 10am - 5pm.

Admission Rates: Adults £7.00, Senior Citizens £5.50, Child £3.50

Groups Rates: Minimum group size 15, Adults £5.00, Child £2.50

Facilities: Visitor Centre, Gift Shop, Plant Sales, Teas, Restaurant, Heated indoor viewing gallery, Gallery housing art and craft exhibitions.

Disabled Access: Yes (Gardens fully accessible). Toilet and parking for disabled on site. Wheelchairs on loan.

Tours/Events: Vehicle-safari with commentary. Daily raptor displays and bird feeding.

Coach Parking: Yes - free

Length of Visit: 3 - 5 Hours

Booking Contact: Brigid Harrison
Pensthorpe Nature Reserve & Gardens, Fakenham, Norfolk, NR21 0LN.
Telephone: 01328 851465   Fax: 01328 855905

Email: info@pensthorpe.com

Website: www.pensthorpe.com

Location: One mile from Fakenham on the A1067 to Norwich.

Please quote this guide when booking

A visit to Sandringham's sixty-acre gardens is a delight at any time of year. Woodland walks, lakes and streams are planted to provide year-round colour and interest; sheets of spring - flowering bulbs, avenues of rhododendrons and azaleas, beds of lavender and roses, dazzling autumn colour - there is always something to see. Other highlights include the formal North Garden, Queen Alexandra's summerhouse beside its own cascading stream, sixteen species of oak and many commemorative trees. Guided garden walks offered regularly.

Open Easter to mid-July and early August to end October, 10.30am to 5pm daily.

Fact File

Opening Times:	Easter - mid July and early August - end October
Admission Rates:	Adults £5.50, Senior Citizen £4.50, Child £3.50.
Groups Rates:	Minimum group size: 20
	10% discount when booked and paid for 30 days prior.
Facilities:	Visitor Centre, Gift Shop, Plant Sales, Teas, Restaurant, Sandringham Museum (inc in ticket)
	Sandringham House (Extra Charge).
Disabled Access:	Yes. Toilet and parking for disabled on site, Wheelchairs on loan.
Tours/Events:	Guided garden walks offered regularly.
Coach Parking:	Yes
Length of Visit:	2 hours. (for Garden only, longer for House and Museum).
Booking Contact:	Mrs N Colman
	Sandringham, Norfolk. PE35 6EN.
	Tel: 01553 612908 Fax: 01485 541571
Email:	visits@sandringhamestate.co.uk
Website:	www.sandringhamestate.co.uk
Location:	8 miles northeast of Kings Lynn on A149.

Please quote this guide when booking

Coton Manor   Northamptonshire

Coton Manor lies in peaceful Northamptonshire countryside providing an ideal setting for the ten acre garden. Originally laid out in the 1920s by the grandparents of the current owner it comprises a number of smaller gardens, each one distinctive, providing variety and interest throughout the season.

The 17th century manor house acts as a central focus for the garden with the walls supporting unusual climbing roses, clematis and shrubs while the surrounding York stone terraces are populated by numerous pots and containers overflowing with pelargoniums, verbenas, heliotropes, salvias and agapanthus. The rest of the garden slopes down from the house and is landscaped on different levels lending a natural informality. Old yew and holly hedges complement the many luxuriant borders packed with unusual plants (most available in the specialist nursery) and displaying inspirational colour schemes throughout the season. Water is abundant at Coton with natural flowing streams, ponds and fountains everywhere. Beyond the confines of the garden there is a magnificent bluebell wood and established wildflower meadow.

The widely respected Good Gardens Guide says of Coton 'This is a beautifully maintained garden of exceptional charm with unexpected vistas at every turn....there is something for everyone here'.

Fact File

Opening Times: 1st April to 30th September. Tues to Sat and Bank Holiday weekends. (Also Sundays in April and May) 12 noon - 5.30pm.

Admission Rates: Adults £4.50, Senior Citizens £4.00, Child £2.00.

Group Rates: Adults £4.00

Facilities: Restaurant available for group bookings. Tearoom serving light lunches and teas, Extensive nursery with many unusual plants mostly grown from the garden. Shop.

Disabled Access: Yes (difficult in places) Toilet and parking for disabled on site.

Tours/Events: Tours by appointment (Wednesdays), Hellebore weekends (early March), Bluebell Wood (early May), Rose week (late June).

Coach Parking: Yes.

Length of Visit: 2 - 2 1/2 hours

Booking Contact: Sarah Ball,
Coton Manor Garden, Nr Guilsborough, Northampton NN6 8RQ.
Telephone: 01604 740219 Fax: 01604 740838

Email: pasleytyler@cotonmanor.fsnet.co.uk

Website: www.cotonmanor.co.uk

Location: 9 miles NW of Northampton, between A5199 (formerly A50) and A428.

Please quote this guide when booking

Huge 300-year-old cedars set off magnificent double herbaceous borders, pools and lily-ponds, whilst on the south front are formal parterres framing the vista towards the famous 7th century church at Brixworth.

There is a stately Yew Statue Walk and many captivating views over the lake and Park. Here too are pergolas, rose borders and individually planted courtyards. In midsummer, visitors enjoy the splendid array of planters, a sight not to be missed.

The magical Wild Garden is a short walk across the Park and is planted along the course of a stream with its small cascades and arched bridges. Here are the wonderful colours of acers and rhododendrons, with bamboos and gunneras.

A number of distinguished landscape designers have been involved with gardens at Cottesbrooke including, Robert Weir Schultz, Sir Geoffrey Jellicoe and Dame Sylvia Crowe.

Fact File

Opening Times: May 1st to the end of September. May & June: Wed & Thurs 2pm - 5.30pm, July, Aug & Sept: Thurs 2pm - 5.30pm, Plus Bank Hol Mondays (May-Sept) 2pm - 5.30pm

Admission Rates: House & Gardens: Adults £7.50, Child £3.50. (5 - 14yrs)
Gardens only: Adults £5.00, Child £2.50 (5 - 14yrs)

Group Rates: Group, private, and concession rates on application.

Facilities: Tearoom, Plant sales, Car park.

Disabled Access: Yes (Gardens only), Toilet and parking for disabled on site.
(Please contact administrator regarding disbled access)

Tours/Events: Guided tour of the house (45 mins), Garden tours by arrangement, groups welcome - please pre book.

Coach Parking: Yes.

Length of Visit: 1 $^1/_2$ hours (Garden) 45 mins (House).

Booking Contact: Via the Administrator on 01604 505 808 or Fax on 01604 505 619
or email enquiries@cottesbrooke.co.uk

Email: enquiries@cottesbrooke.co.uk

Website: www.cottesbrookehall.co.uk

Location: Cottesbrooke is situated 10 miles north of Northampton off the A5199. Easily accessible from the A14 (junction 1 - A5199) and M1/M6.

Please quote this guide when booking

Kelmarsh Hall & Gardens   Northamptonshire

Built in 1732 to a James Gibbs design, Kelmarsh Hall is surrounded by its working estate, grazed parkland and twentieth century gardens. The gardens are largely attributed to Nancy Lancaster who, in the 1920s and 30s, as a tenant in the Hall and married to Ronald Tree, worked with Norah Lindsay laying out the flowerbeds in the topiary garden and in the long border. It was probably through her that Geoffrey Jellico became involved at Kelmarsh in 1936-8 when he laid out the terraced walks, pleached limes and red horse chestnuts on the west front for Colonel Lancaster. In 1948 she returned to Kelmarsh as Nancy Lancaster and continued to develop her style both in the house and in the gardens. Now after seven years of restoration the gardens, with their billowing box hedges, old roses and lavish herbaceous borders, once again reflect that style.

Fact File

Opening Times:	16th April – End of September: Gardens: Tuesdays, Wednesdays, Thursdays and Sundays: 2 p.m. – 5.30 p.m. Hall and Gardens: Bank Holiday Sundays and Mondays and 1st Sunday of every month plus Thursday May - August: 2 p.m. - 5.30 p.m.
Admission Rates:	Garden: Adults £3.50, Senior Citizens £3.00, Children £2.00 House and Gardens: Adults: £4.50 Senior Citizens: £4.00 Children: £2.50
Groups Rates:	Garden: 12; House and Gardens: 17 Adults/Senior Citizens/Children: £5.50
Facilities:	Visitor Centre, Plant Sales, Teas. Toilet and car parking on site.
Disabled Access:	Yes.
Tours/Events:	Guided tours available.
Coach Parking:	Yes
Length of Visit:	2 Hours
Booking Contact:	Lesley Denton, Administrator, Kelmarsh Hall, Kelmarsh, Northampton NN6 9LY Telephone: 01604 686543 Fax: 01604 686437
Email:	enquiries@kelmarsh.com
Website:	www.kelmarsh.com
Location:	5 miles south of Market Harborough on the A508, 1 mile north of junction 2 of the A14.

Please quote this guide when booking

Home of the Isham family for over 400 years. The gardens were originally laid out in 1655 by Gilbert Clark. In the 1820's Mary Isham planted the cedars and was responsible for much of the planting in the surrounding parkland. Mary's son Charles is responsible for the present day appearance with a small Italian garden, complete with shell fountain, and the remarkable rock garden, rising like a ruin 24' tall, which he peopled with small figures, the first garden gnomes in England.

There are also good herbaceous borders, an 18th century box bower, Irish yews and wisteria planted in the 1840's, a privy garden re-created for the 21st century.

Hall entry is included in the ticket price with guided tours on all but fair days.

Fact File

Opening Times: Sundays and Bank Holiday Mondays Easter to 15th October.
Private groups by arrangement at other times.
Admission Rates: (Hall and Gardens): Adults: £5.50, Senior Citizens: £5.00, Children (5-16): £2.00
Group Rates: (private visit): Minimum charge £150
Facilities: Teas, Farm Museum.
Disabled Access: Yes, partial. Toilet and car parking on site.
Tours/Events: Telephone for details.
Coach Parking: Yes, by appointment only.
Length of Visit: Up to 2½ hours, including Hall.
Booking Contact Mrs. Almond, Lamport Hall, Lamport, Northampton, NN6 9HD.
Telephone: 01604 686272 Fax: 01604 686224
Email: admin@lamporthall.co.uk
Website: www.lamporthall.co.uk
Location: On A508 between Northampton and Market Harborough.

Please quote this guide when booking

The Alnwick Garden

Northumberland

The Alnwick Garden is one of the great wonders of the contemporary gardening world. The centrepiece is the Grand Cascade, a magnificent tumbling mass of water, ending in an eruption of fountains sending 350 litres of water into the air every second. A computer system synchronises four sensational displays that offer not only a visual treat but also an interactive experience for children who can play in the water jets.

Beyond this lies the Ornamental Garden, a symmetrical, structured garden with a strong European influence containing 16,500 plants. Nestled in a corner of The Garden is the Rose Garden, with pergola lined paths covered in climbing and shrub roses mixed with glorious honeysuckle and clematis. The Garden is also home to one of the largest wooden tree houses in the world with rope bridges and walkways in the sky. There's also the Serpent Garden, with a wonderful array of water features and topiary, the Bamboo Labyrinth and the intriguing Poison Garden. New for 2006 is the Pavilion and Visitor Centre, magnificent contemporary buildings.

Designed by the renowned Belgium father and son company, Wirtz international, The Garden is the vision of the Duchess of Northumberland.

Fact File

Opening Times: 10am until dusk, every day except Christmas Day.

Admission Rates: Adults £6.00, Senior Citizen £5.75, Children (16 years and under) free when accompanied by an adult (up to 4 children per adult). Prices valid until 20th March 2006.

Groups Rates: Minimum group size: 14
Adults £5.50, Children (16 years and under) free when accompanied by an adult (up to 4 children per adult).

Facilities: Treehouse restaurant and Treehouse Shop. New facilities for 2006 in Pavilion and Visitor Centre

Disabled Access: Yes. Toilet and parking for disabled on site.

Tours/Events: Please telephone 01665 511350 for details of tours and special events.

Coach Parking: Yes

Length of Visit: At least 2 hours

Booking Contact: The Alnwick Garden, Alnwick, Northumberland, NE66 1YU
Telephone: 01665 511350 Fax: 01665 511351

Email: info@alnwickgarden.com

Website: www.alnwickgarden.com

Location: Leave the A1 North of the town at the junction signposted by the tourist information sign for The Alnwick Garden. The Garden is clearly signposted, approx 1 mile from the A1 junction.

Please quote this guide when booking

Cragside has one of the finest high Victorian gardens in the country open to visitors. The rock garden is one of the largest in Europe and is probably the last surviving example of its type. Later in 2006 and following major restoration work, the water cascades will be in full use for the first time in over 75 years. (Please ring for details).

A fine collection of conifers, mainly from North America, is to be found in the Pinetum, below Cragside House, and across the valley lie the three terraces of the Formal Garden. On the top terrace is the Orchard House, the only remaining glass house in the gardens, which was built for the culture of early fruit. Nearby are the stone-framed carpet beds, planted for the summer season and on the middle terrace just below is the Dahlia Walk. Restoration has just been completed on the bottom, or Italian Terrace, which contains a wonderful loggia and an imposing quatre-foil pool. Finally, the Valley Garden itself is yet to be developed, but provides a wonderful setting for a gentle stroll.

Fact File

Opening Times: 1st April - 29th October, Tuesday - Sunday (and Bank Holiday Mondays).
Gardens & Estate: 10.30am - 7.00pm or dusk if earlier (Last admission 5.00pm).
Please note the House will be closed throughout 2006 for rewiring.
Winter 1 Nov - 17 Dec Wed - Sun 11.00am - 4.00pm (last admission 3pm) House closed.

Admission Rates: Gardens & Estate - Adults £6.50, Child £3.00 (5-17yrs), Family £16.00 (2 adults + 3 child)
Winter - Adults £3.00, Child £1.50 (5-17yrs), Family £7.50 (2 adults + 3 child)
Special offer Nov and Dec - spend £10 in the shop or restaurant and have admission refunded

Group Rates: Minimum group size 15: must be pre-booked.
Gardens & Estate: £4.50, Winter £2.00

Facilities: Visitor Centre, Shop, Restaurant.

Disabled Access: Limited. Please ring to discuss.

Tours/Events: Tours by private arrangement subject to availability. Please telephone for events programme.

Coach Parking: Yes   **Length of Visit:** minimum 3 hours

Booking Contact: Val Miller. Cragside, Rothbury, Morpeth, Northumberland, NE65 7PX
Telephone: 01669 622001 Fax: 01669 620066

Email: val.miller@nationaltrust.org.uk   **Website:** www.nationaltrust.org.uk

Location: Entrance 1 mile N of Rothbury (B6341). 15 miles NW of Morpeth, 13 miles SW of Alnwick.

Please quote this guide when booking

Buscot Park  Oxfordshire

In 2004 *Country Life* Magazine voted Buscot Park one of the best water gardens in England. The Water Garden was laid out by Harold Peto in 1904 for the 1st Lord Faringdon. Peto was the leading exponent of formal Italianate garden design of his day and intended the Water Garden to create a link between the eighteenth century house and the lake.

Designed as a descending canal between woods on either side, it is carved out within a grass walkway, lined with box hedges which widen at intervals to allow the canal to expand into formal rectangular pools. Statues, seats and fastigiate yews flank the hedges and the descent is punctuated by stone steps, footbridges and occasional fountains. Elsewhere in the park the present Lord Faringdon continues to enhance the landscape and has recently transformed the redundant kitchen gardens into the Four Seasons walled garden approached through colourful year-round borders planted by Peter Coates in 1986.

Photo of Peto Water Garden by David Dixon

Fact File

Opening Times: Please Call 0845 345 3387 for details or visit website. (3rd April - 29th Sept)
Admission Rates: Adults £7.00 (House & Gardens) £5.00 (Gardens Only), Child 1/2 Adult price.
Group Rates: None
Facilities: Teas, Occasional plant sales. Self pick soft fruit in season - tel 01367 245705.
Disabled Access: Partial, adapted WC's and ramps in gardens/tearoom. Two single seater powered mobility vehicles can be booked in advance.
Tours/Events: None
Coach Parking: Yes.
Length of Visit: 3 hours
Booking Contact: Estate Office
Buscot Park, Faringdon, Oxfordshire, SN7 8BU.
Telephone: 01367 240786 Fax: 01367 241794
Email: estbuscot@aol.com
Website: www.buscot-park.com
Location: Buscot Park is on the A417 between Faringdon and Lechlade. It is marked on most larger scale road maps.

Please quote this guide when booking

Cotswold Wildlife Park & Gardens Oxfordshire

Following extensive developments the Park has become an unexpected attraction to gardeners. Always a family favourite with animal lovers, garden lovers are surprised at the rich diversity of plants and planting styles encountered throughout the 160 acres of landscaped parkland surrounding a listed Victorian Manor House. The Victorian residents would have been familiar with formal parterres and traditional herbaceous borders but not the exuberant and stunning summer displays of hardy and tender exotics including huge bananas and flamboyant cannas now found in what was once the Walled Kitchen Garden. The unique arid-scape of cactus and succulents surrounding the meerkats, the calls of Kookaburras, Lemurs and Macaws give this area a truly tropical ambience. The flower meadows of snowdrops, narcissus and bluebells, so welcome in the spring, contrast with the large sweeping groups of ornamental grasses and perennials which provide a wonderful foil for rhino and zebras and the many different types of bamboo which feature strongly in other animal enclosures.

Fact File

Opening Times: Everyday (except Christmas Day). 10am.
(last admission 3.30pm October - February).

Admission Rates: Adults £9.00, Senior Citizens £6.50, Child £6.50, (3-16yrs).

Group Rates: Minimum group size: 20
Adults £7.50, Senior Citizen £5.50, Child £5.00.

Facilities: Shop, Teas, Restaurant.
(Restaurant available for booked lunches and teas, waitress service in Orangery).

Disabled Access: Yes. Parking for disabled on site. Wheelchairs on loan, booking necessary.

Tours/Events: Gardens Special for inclusive charge, talk by Head Gardener or his Deputy in the Drawing room of the Manor House and Cotswold Cream Teas in the Orangery.

Coach Parking: Yes

Length of Visit: 2 1/2 - 3 hours

Booking Contact: General Office. Cotswold Wildlife Park, Burford, Oxfordshire, OX18 4JW
Telephone: 01993 823006 Fax: 01993 823807

Email: None

Website: www.cotswoldwildlifepark.co.uk

Location: On A361 2.5 miles south of A40 at Burford.

ROUSHAM and its landscape garden should be a place of pilgrimage for students of the work of William Kent (1685 - 1748).

Rousham represents the first phase of English landscape design and remains almost as Kent left it, one of the few gardens of this date to have escaped alteration, with many features which delighted eighteenth century visitors to Rousham still in situ.

The house, built in 1635 by Sir Robert Dormer, is still in the ownership of the same family. Kent added the wings and the stable block. Don't miss the walled garden with their herbacious borders, small parterre, pigeon house and espalier trees. A fine herd of rare Long-Horn cattle are to be seen in the park.

Rousham is uncommercial and unspoilt with no tea room and no shop. Bring a picnic, wear comfortable shoes and its yours for the day.

Fact File

Opening Times:	Every Day All Year
Admission Rates:	Adults £4.00, Senior Citizen £4.00, No Children under 15.
Groups Rates:	None
Facilities:	None
Disabled Access:	Partial, parking for disabled on site.
Tours/Events:	None
Coach Parking:	Yes
Length of Visit:	1 - 2 hours.
Booking Contact:	C Cottrell - Dormer
	Rousham, Nr Steeple Aston, Bicester, Oxon, OX25 4QX.
	Tel: 01869 347110 Fax: 01869 347110
Email:	None
Website:	www.rousham.org
Location:	South of B4030, East of A4260.

Sulgrave Manor is a superb example of a modest manor house and garden of the time of Shakespeare, and was home to the ancestors of George Washington, the first President of the United States of America. In 1539 the manor was bought from Henry VIII by Lawrence Washington, and his descendants were to live there for the next 120 years. Sulgrave Manor was presented by British subscribers to the peoples of Great Britain and the United States of America in celebration of the Hundred Years Peace between the two nations. In 1924, the National Society of the Colonial Dames of America generously endowed the Manor House, and still co-operate with the board in its upkeep. Today visitors from all over the world, including many school children, come to enjoy this beautiful Tudor House set within the heart of a peaceful Northamptonshire village. The many attractions include the new Elizabethan Hangings. The individual designs have been embroidered by more than 500 volunteers from both Great Britain and the United States of America. Some motifs directly relevant to the sixteenth century.

Fact File

Opening Times:	Weekends April - October 12.00 - 4.00 last entry.
	Tuesday, Wednesday, Thursday May - October 2.00 - 4.00 last entry.
Admission Rates:	Adults £5.75, Child £2.50,
Group Rates:	Minimum group size: 15
	Adults Variable
Facilities:	Gift Shop, Cafe
Disabled Access:	Partial. Toilet for disabled on site.
Tours/Events:	Yes, Please call for details
Coach Parking:	Yes
Length of Visit:	2 hours
Booking Contact:	Cheryl Moss
	Sulgrave Manor, Sulgrave, Banbury, OX17 2SD
	Telephone: 01295 760205 Fax: 01295 768056
Email:	sulgrave-manor@talk21.com
Website:	www.sulgravemanor.org.uk
Location:	Follow brown tourist signs from A43, M40 or M1

Please quote this guide when booking

Upton House and Gardens   Oxfordshire

Discover 32 acres of magnificent gardens set in unspoilt countryside on the Warwickshire-Oxfordshire border. Created from two spring-fed valleys on the Edge Hill plateau, the gardens have been in use since the 12th Century, but were largely transformed by Kitty Lloyd-Jones in the 1920's and 30's, with the creation of cascading terraces on the valley sides, extensive herbaceous borders, and a rare Bog Garden on the site of medieval fish ponds. The gardens provide today's visitors with a variety of experiences, including large lawns, terraced borders, elegant stone staircases, rose garden, orchards, and a rare kitchen display garden.

A highlight is the National Collection of Aster amellus, Aster cordifolius, and Aster ericoïdes, providing sumptuous colour in early autumn.

At the heart of the site is the 17th century mansion, extended and remodelled in the 1920s for the 2nd Viscount Bearsted as a weekend retreat, and as a gallery for his incredible art collection, regarded as one of the nation's most important private collections of the 20th century.

Fact File

Opening Times:	Monday – Wednesday: 12noon – 5pm Saturday, Sunday, Bank Holidays: 11am – 5pm
Admission Rates:	Adults: £7.00 (£4.20 garden only) National Trust Members: Free
	Children: £3.70 (£2.10 garden only)
Group Rates:	Minimum group size: 15
	Adults: £5.60 (£3.50 garden only)
Facilities:	Visitor Centre, Shop, Plant Sales, Restaurant, Teas, Free car parking,
	Bookable holiday cottage in garden.
Disabled Access:	Yes – partial. Toilet and car parking on site. Wheelchair loan available please book.
Tours/Events:	Jazz concerts, Aster open days, lecture lunches, 1920s days, vintage car meetings, art days
	art workshops, Christmas opening.
Coach Parking:	Yes
Length of Visit:	3 hours
Booking Contact	Jane Scarff, Upton House & Gardens, Upton House, Banbury, Oxfordshire OX15 6HT.
	Telephone 01295 670266 Fax: 01295 671144
Email:	uptonhouse@nationaltrust.org.uk
Website:	www.nationaltrust.org.uk
Location:	On the A422 between Banbury and Stratford upon Avon. Signposted from Junction 12 M40.
	Nearest station: Banbury (7 miles).

Please quote this guide when booking

Waterperry Gardens   Oxfordshire

The magnificent gardens at Waterperry are within easy reach of Oxford and for the visitor, this is a chance to share and enjoy the beauty and peace of this truly special place. This 3.2 Ha (8-acre) garden contains one of the best purely herbaceous borders in the country, which flowers from May until November. There is however so much more to interest the garden visitor throughout the year; including rose and alpine gardens, a knot garden, trained fruit and nursery beds as well as a pleasant riverside walk. The plant centre sells plants of the very highest quality, which are mainly grown at Waterperry. There is always a large choice of herbaceous perennials, shrubs and in-season fruit trees. The shop sells a full range of garden sundries as well as a wonderful range of gifts and there is a well-stocked bookshop. British arts and crafts can be seen and purchased from the Art in Action gallery. There is also a small but interesting museum of rural life and the Saxon church is also worth a visit. The teashop serves homemade lunches and teas, made with fresh local ingredients, which can be enjoyed inside or out on our spacious lawns.

Fact File

Opening Times: April - October - 9am - 5.30pm, November - March 9am - 5pm.
Admission Rates: Adults £4.25, Senior Citizens £3.75, Child £3.00 under 10's Free. (Nov - Mar all £3.00)
Group Rates: Minimum group size: 20+ booked in advance.
Adults £3.25, Senior Citizens £3.25, Child £2.50, under 10's Free.
Facilities: Garden Shop, Plant Sales, Teas, Restaurant, Art in Action Gallery, Museum.
Disabled Access: Yes. Toilet and parking for disabled on site. Wheelchairs on loan.
Tours/Events: Tours can be arranged
Snowdrop Weekend 12th-13th February, Aster Weekend 23th-24th September,
Apple Weekend 14th - 15th October.
Coach Parking: Yes
Length of Visit: Approx 3 - 4 hours
Booking Contact: Main Office, Waterperry Gardens, Nr Wheatley, Oxon, OX33 1JZ
Telephone: 01844 339254 Fax: 01844 339883
Email: office@waterperrygardens.co.uk
Website: www.waterperrygardens.co.uk
Location: 7 miles east of Oxford - junction 8 M40 from London. Follow brown signs.
Junction 8a from Birmingham.

Please quote this guide when booking

Barnsdale Gardens   Rutland

The Barnsdale Garden familiar to millions of BBC2 viewers as the home of Geoff Hamilton and Gardeners' World comprises of 37 individual gardens and features that all blend together by the linking borders into one 8 acre garden.

There is not only a wealth of different plants to come and see, in many different conbinations, but also an enormous amount of practical ideas for any gardener. On average most people spend about 3 hours in the garden before venturing over to the nursery where we sell a wide range of choice and unusual garden plants, many initially propagated from the gardens. So allow plenty of time to take it all in and then relax in our small and friendly licensed coffee shop which serves a very appetising range of hot and cold food and drink.

We look forward to seeing you.

Fact File

Opening Times: March- May, September & October 9am - 5pm. June - August 9am - 7pm, November - February 10am - 4pm. (Last entry 2 hours prior to closing). Closed 22nd and 25th December.

Admission Rates: Adults £6.00, Senior Citizen £5.00, Child £2.00. Family Ticket £15.00 (2 Adults + 3 child)

Groups Rate: Minimum group size: 11
Adults £4.50, Senior Citizen £4.50, Child £1.50.

Facilities: Shop, Tea Room, Plant Sales.

Disabled Access: Yes. Toilet and parking for disabled on site. Wheelchairs on loan, booking advisable.

Tours/Events: Yes throughout the year. Courses and Events booklet available.

Coach Parking: Yes

Length of Visit: 3 hours

Booking Contact: Barnsdale Gardens, The Avenue, Exton, Oakham, Rutland, LE15 8AH
Telephone: 01572 813200 Fax: 01572 813346

Email: marketing@barnsdalegardens.co.uk

Website: www.barnsdalegardens.co.uk

Location: AC0C Oakham to Stamford and turn off at Barnsdale Lodge Hotel and we are then 1 mile on the left.

Please quote this guide when booking

Set amongst glorious views of the Staffordshire countryside this beautiful garden, created by local landowner, Colonel Harry Clive for his wife Dorothy, embraces a varity of landscape features. They include a superb woodland garden etched from a disused gravel quarry, an alpine scree, a fine collection of specimen trees, spectacular summer flower borders and many rare and unusual plants to intrigue and delight.

A host of spring bulbs, magnificent displays of Rhododendrons and Azaleas and stunning autumn colour are among the seasonal highlights.

A fine tearoom, overlooking the garden, provides a selection of home baking and light lunches.

Fact File

Opening Times: Saturday 11th March - Tuesday 31st October.
Admission Rates: Adults £4.20, Senior Citizen £3.60, Child (11-16) £1.00, up to 11 Free.
Group Rates: Minimum group size: 20
Daytime £3.60, Evening £4.20
Facilities: Teas
Disabled Access: Yes, Toilet and parking for disabled on site. Wheelchairs on loan, booking necessary.
Tours/Events: None
Coach Parking: Yes.
Length of Visit: 1 1/2 hours
Booking Contact: The Secretary
The Dorothy Clive Garden, Willoughbridge, Market Drayton, Shropshire, TF9 4EU
Telephone: 01630 647237 Fax: 01630 647902
Email: info@dorothyclivegarden.co.uk
Website: www.dorothyclivegarden.co.uk
Location: On the A51, two miles south from the village of Woore. From the M6 leave at Junction 15, take the A53, then the A51

Please quote this guide when booking

Wollerton Old Hall Garden   Shropshire

Created 20 years ago around a Tudor house (not open), this quality garden has achieved the highest "Good Garden Guide" rating and RHS Partnership status. Designed by the owner, Lesley Jenkins, this outstanding garden combines a strong structure with clever planting combinations using perennials.

The early spring shows of anemones, hellebores and trilliums are followed by tulips, aquilegias and oriental poppies. The summer roses herald the arrival of the delphiniums which in turn give way to the dominance of stately hollyhocks and vibrant phlox. August sees the hot garden ignited which still burns when the asters and euonymus seed capsules arrive in September.

The garden has significant collections of rare perennials, salvias, paniculata phlox and clematis and many of these are available in the Plant Centre. The Tea Room provides excellent lunches, teas and evening meals with all the food being prepared freshly on the premises.

Fact File

Opening Times:	Public days – Good Friday, every Friday, Sunday and Bank Holiday until end of September: 12 noon – 5 p.m.
Admission Rates:	Adults/Senior Citizens: £4 per person, Children 4-15 years: £1.
Group Rates:	Garden groups welcome by appointment on Tuesdays and Wednesdays.
Facilities:	Plant Sales, Lunches, Teas, large car park for cars.
Disabled Access:	Easy wheelchair access for 80% of the garden. The remainder accessible with helper.
Tours/Events:	Guided tours available: topic-specific garden tours with Head Gardener. Lectures by garden personalities. Evening Summer Strolls with candlelit garden and salmon supper.
Coach Parking:	Coaches welcome by appointment. Coach parking available on the lane outside the garden.
Length of Visit:	2 – 4 hours, depending upon level of plant interest.
Booking Contact	Diana Oakes. Wollerton Old Hall Garden, Wollerton, Market Drayton, TF9 3NA. Telephone: 01630 685760 Fax: 01630 685583
Email:	info@wollertonoldhallgarden.com
Website:	www.wollertonoldhallgarden.com
Location:	The garden is brown-signed off the A53 between the A41 junction and Hodnet.

Please quote this guide when booking

The American Museum in Britain

Located in an area of outstanding natural beauty, the hilltop site of Claverton Manor, the home of the American Museum, takes full advantage of the spectacular views over the valley of the River Avon. The grounds total some 120 acres of which forty are open to visitors. A unique replica of George Washington's flower garden at Mount Vernon, Virginia is flanked by an Arboretum devoted to American trees and shrubs. Below this has been added the Lewis and Clark trail containing trees and shrubs discovered on the pioneering expedition across the States, now celebrating its 200th anniversary. The parkland, with its majestic old cedars, provides a circular walk through ancient meadows while above the house a path has been created through woodland. A small vegetable garden dye plant area and colonial herb garden give a flavour of early colonial plantings.

Fact File

Opening Times:	Mid March to end October: Tuesday – Sunday (Bank Holiday Mondays and during August) 12.00noon – 5.00pm
Admission Rates:	Adults: £4.00/£6.50. Senior Citizens: £3.50/£6.00. Children: £2.50/£3.50
Group Rates:	Minimum Groups Size: 20. Adults/Senior Citizens: £5.00 (House & Garden ticket only).
Facilities:	Shop. Plant sales. Restaurant. Teas. Museum of American Decorative Art.
Disabled Access:	Limited disabled access. Toilet and parking on site.
Tours/Events:	Guided tours available. Visit website: www.americanmuseum.org for details on special events.
Coach Parking:	Yes.
Length of Visit:	$1^{1}/_{2}$ - 2 hours
Booking Contact	Helen Hayden. The American Museum in Britain, Claverton Manor, Bath, Somerset, BA2 7BD Telephone: 01225 460503 Fax: 01225 469160
Email:	info@americanmuseum.org
Website:	www.americanmuseum.org
Location:	Just along from the University of Bath. Signposted from Bath City Centre and A36 Warminster Road. Coaches MUST approach from city centre, up Bathwick Hill.

Please quote this guide when booking

Barrington Court   Somerset

The enchanting formal garden, influenced greatly by Gertrude Jekyll, is laid out in a series of walled rooms, and includes the White Garden, Rose and Iris Garden and the stunning Lily Garden. There is also a Tudor manor house.

Running along the outer border of the Kitchen Garden to the hip roofed 1920s Squash Court is the Herbaceous Border, containing, amongst others, the magnificent Onopordon in the middle and asters, Helenium and Alcea rosea at the back. The Pergola Walk is covered by climbing honeysuckle, wisteria, hop and clematises such as 'Perle d'Azur'.

The extremely picturesque bustalls, red brick sheds originally for calf rearing, are now festooned with roses such as 'Sympathie'.

The working kitchen garden, which supplies the restaurant, has espaliered apples, pears, and plums along high stone walls. Alongside nectarines and peaches are other plants such as cardoons, figs, liquorice and sesame.

Fact File

Opening Times: 2 – 31 March 2006: 11.00am – 4.30pm Thursday, Friday, Saturday, Sunday.
1 April – 30 September 2006: 11.00am – 5.30pm every day except Wednesday.
1 – 31 October: 11.00am – 4.30pm, Thursday, Friday, Saturday and Sunday.

Admission Rates: Adults: £7.00. Senior Citizens: £7.00. Children (5 16) £3.00

Group Rates: Minimum Groups Size: 15. Adults: £6.00. Senior Citizens: £6.00. Children £3.00

Facilities: Shop. Plant Sales. Restaurant. Teas. Elizabethan manor house included in ticket price.

Disabled Access: Yes. Toilet and parking on site. Wheelchair Loan booking available.

Tours/Events: Guided tours available. Please telephone 01460 242614 for details on special events.

Coach Parking: Yes.

Length of Visit: 2 hours

Booking Contact Margaret Stone. Barrington Court, Nr. Ilminster, Somerset, TA19 0NQ
Telephone: 01460 242614 Fax: 01460 243133

Email: Margaret.stone@nationaltrust.org.uk

Website: www.nationaltrust.org.uk

Location: In Barrington village, 5 miles NE of Ilminster, on B3168. Signposted from A358 (Ilminster – Taunton) and A303 (Hayes End roundabout).

Please quote this guide when booking

Cothay Manor and Gardens

Somerset

Five miles West of Wellington, hidden in the high-banked lanes of Somerset, lies Cothay, built at the end of the Wars of the Roses in 1485. Virtually unchanged in 500 years, this sleeping beauty sits on the banks of the river Tone within its twelve acres of magical Gardens.

The Gardens, laid out in the 1920's, have been re-designed and replanted within the original structure. Many garden rooms, each a garden in itself, are set off a 200 yard yew walk. In addition there is a bog garden with azaleas and drifts of primuli, a cottage garden, a courtyard garden, river walk and fine trees. A truly romantic plantsman's paradise. **Two stars in the Good Garden Guide.**

Picture taken by; Christopher Simon Sykes

Fact File

Opening Times: May to September incl. Wed, Thurs, Sun & Bank Holidays - 2pm to 6pm.

Admission Rates: Gardens only - Adults £4.50, Senior Citizens £4.50, Child (under 12) £2.00.

Group Rates: Minimum group size: 20+
Please contact us for information pack. All groups by appointment only.

Facilities: Plant Sales, Cream Teas, (Groups 20+ catering by arrangement).

Disabled Access: Yes (Garden) Partial (House), Toilet and parking for disabled on site.

Tours/Events: **Groups only:** Guided Garden Tour lasting one hour.
Guided house tour 1 1/2hrs. **The Manor is open to groups throughout the year.**

Coach Parking: Yes.

Length of Visit: 1 1/2 - 3 1/2 hours

Booking Contact: The Administrator
Cothay Manor, Greenham, Wellington, Somerset, TA21 0JR
Telephone: 01823 672 283 Fax: 01823 672 345

Email: cothaymanor@realemail.co.uk

Website: None

Location: From junction 26 M5, direction Wellington, take A38 direction Exeter, 31/2 miles turn right to Greenham. From junction 27 M5 take A38 direction Wellington, 31/2 miles take 2nd turning left to Greenham.

Please quote this guide when booking

East Lambrook Manor Gardens   Somerset

East Lambrook Manor is recognised internationally as the 'Home of English Cottage Gardening'. This famous Grade I listed garden was created by the gardening icon, Margery Fish, in the 1950s and is home to many rare and unusual native plants, many of which she saved from virtual extinction. Margery Fish's Plant nursery remains today, with the gardeners still taking cuttings from the garden to propagate an exciting selection of plants for sale. The nursery continues to house a wonderful hardy geranium collection. The tea shop has won the top award in Somerset for the last 3 years and specialises in homemade and local West Country foods. There is also an art gallery and a wonderful gift shop. The garden opens 10am to 5pm daily from 1st February for the stunning snowdrop displays, and then closes on 31st October.

Fact File

Opening Times:	1st February to 31st October: 10am to 5pm daily, including all Bank Holidays.
Admission Rates:	Adults: £3.95. Senior Citizens: £3.50. Children: Free.
Group Rates:	Minimum Groups Size: 10. Adults: £3.50. Senior Citizens: £3.50
Facilities:	Visitor Centre, Shop, Plant sales, Restaurant, Teas, Art Gallery
Disabled Access:	Semi. Toilet and car parking on site.
Tours/Events:	Talk by head gardener available. Various. Events for 2006 to be confirmed (see website).
Coach Parking:	Yes.
Length of Visit:	Any time.
Booking Contact	Marianne Williams – owner
	East Lambrook Manor, South Petherton, Somerset, TA13 5HH
	Telephone: 01460 240328 Fax: 01460 242344
Email:	office@eastlambrook.com
Website:	www.eastlambrook.com
Location:	A303 in Somerset. Turn off at South Petherton and follow brown flower signs into East Lambrook village.

Please quote this guide when booking

Forde Abbey & Gardens Dorset

One of the top ten gardens in England surrounds a magnificent 12th century home. Built of golden Hamstone it is a beautiful backdrop for a fascinating garden which has its beginnings in the early 1700's and was one of the first landscaped gardens. Throughout the seasons each area has its moment of glory. The acres of Crocus, the Azaleas and Rhododendrons, the spectacular Bog garden, the colourful rock garden, and the series of cascades and ponds with the Ionic Temple serenely overlooking the herbaceous borders.

The walled kitchen garden supplies the restaurant and house with fresh vegetables and salads, and the year finishes with the beautiful autumn colours in the arboretum. Wherever you are in the garden you can glimpse the spectacular Centenery Fountain, the highest powered fountain in England.

Forde Abbey is a remarkable place, with its combination of grandeur and simplicity, the quality of timelessness and of total sympathy with the countryside around, making it a unique garden with something of interest to everyone.

Fact File

Opening Times: Gardens open daily throughout the year from 10am (last admission 4.30pm). House open 2nd April to end of October, 12noon-4pm on Tue -Fri, Sundays & Bank Holiday Mondays.

Admission Rates: Tel: 01460 221290

Groups Rates: Minimum group size 20, Tel: 01460 220231.

Facilities: Visitor Centre, Shop, Plant Sales, Teas, Restaurant and Pottery Exhibition.

Disabled Access: Yes. (house not suitable for wheelchairs) Toilet and parking for disabled on site. Wheelchairs on loan, booking necessary.

Tours/Events: None

Coach Parking: Yes

Length of Visit: 3 hours

Booking Contact: Mrs Carolyn Clay
Forde Abbey, Chard, TA20 4LU
Telephone: 01460 220231 Fax: 01460 220296

Email: info@fordeabbey.net

Website: www.fordeabbey.co.uk

Location: Signposted from A30 Chard to Crewkerne & from A358 Chard to Axminster.
4 miles south east of Chard.

Please quote this guide when booking

Hestercombe Gardens

Somerset

Lose yourself in 40 acres of walks, streams and temples, vivid colours, formal terraces, woodland, lakes, cascades and views that take your breath away.

This is Hestercombe: a unique combination of three period gardens. The Georgian landscaped garden was created in the 1750's by Coplestone Warre Bampfylde, whose vision was complemented by the addition of a Victorian terrace and Shrubbery and the stunning Edwardian gardens designed by Sir Edwin Lutyens and Gertrude Jekyll. All once abandoned, now being faithfully restored to their former glory: each garden has its own quality of tranqility, wonder and inspiration.

Fact File

Opening Times:	Open every day 10am - 6pm (last admissions 5pm).
Admission Rates:	Adults £6.00, Senior Citizen £5.50, Child (5-15yrs) 2 Free with each paying adult.
Group Rates:	Minimum group size: 20
	Adults £4.90
Facilities:	Visitor Centre with Courtyard Cafe, Shop, Plant Sales. Function Rooms.
Disabled Access:	Partial. Toilet & parking for disabled on site. Wheelchairs on loan, booking not required.
Tours/Events:	A wide range of events including Open Air Plays, Gift Fayre and many other seasonal events. Walks. Garden tours available for groups.
Coach Parking:	Yes
Length of Visit:	2 hours
Booking Contact:	Mrs Jackie Manning
	Hestercombe Gardens, Cheddon Fitzpaine, Taunton, Somerset, TA2 8LG
	Telephone 01823 413923 Fax: 01823 413747
Email:	info@hestercombegardens.com
Website:	www.hestercombegardens.com
Location:	4 miles from Taunton, Signposted from all main roads with the Tourist Information Daisy symbol.

Please quote this guide when booking

Prior Park Landscape Garden   Somerset

Beautiful and intimate 18th century landscaped garden, created by local entrepreneur and philanthropist Ralph Allen with advice from the poet Alexander Pope and 'Capability' Brown, the garden is set in a sweeping valley with magnificent views of the City of Bath. Some of the interesting features are a Palladian bridge, three lakes, and the summerhouse. An ideal picnic location.

The Wilderness is in the final stage of restoration, this includes the Serpentine Lake and water cascades, Gothic Temple and Cabinet. A 5-minute walk from the garden leads on to the Bath Skyline, a 6 mile walk with views of the city.

There is no car parking at the garden, public transport runs to and from the garden every 15 minutes. Call for a 'How to get There' leaflet or down load a copy from the website.

Fact File

Opening Times: 2nd Feb - 30th Nov 11am - 5.30pm every day except Tuesdays.
1st Dec - 30th Jan 11am - Dusk Fri, Sat, Sunday. (Closed 25th,26th Dec & Jan 1st)

Admission Rates: Adults £4.50, Child £2.50, Family Ticket (2 Adults,2 Children) £11.50 (NT members free).

Facilities: Refreshments weekends April - September.

Disabled Access: Partial. Toilet and parking for disabled on site, call to book disabled parking.

Tours/Events: Events programme, call for details.

Coach Parking: No

Length of Visit: 1 1/2 hours

Booking Contact: Visitor Services Manager
Prior Park Landscape Garden, Ralph Allen Drive, Bath, Somerset, BA2 5AH
Telephone: 01225 833422 Fax: 01225 833422

Email: priorpark@nationaltrust.org.uk

Website: www.nationaltrust.org.uk/priorpark

Location: The Garden is a 30 minute walk from Bath city centre.

Please quote this guide when booking

Loseley Park   Surrey

Part of the magnificent grounds of Loseley Park, the original two and a half acre Walled Garden is largely based on a design by Gertrude Jekyll.

The Walled Garden features five exquisite gardens, each with its own theme and character. The award-winning Rose Garden is planted with over one thousand bushes, mainly old-fashioned varieties. The extensive Herb Garden contains four separate sections devoted to culinary, medicinal, household and ornamental. The Fruit and Flower Garden is designed to provide interest and bold fiery colour throughout the season. The White Garden, in total contrast, is planted with white, cream and silver plants, with two water features, creating an idyllic and tranquil area. And the latest addition is the spectacular Organic Vegetable Garden. Other features include the magnificent vine walk, mulberry trees, ancient wisteria and moat which runs almost the entire length of the Walled Garden and is abundant with wildlife and pond plants.
New for 2006 - wild flower meadow.

Fact File

Opening Times:	Gardens open: May - September, Tuesday - Sunday 11am - 5pm. (Loseley House open for guided tours: May - August, Tues - Thurs & Sun, 1pm - 5pm) Separate admission charge. May and August Bank Holidays.
Admission Rates:	Adults £4.00, Senior Citizen £3.50, Child £2.00
Groups Rates:	Minimum group size: 10 Adults £3.00, Child £1.50
Facilities:	Lunchtime Restaurant, Courtyard Teas, Shop, Plant Sales.
Disabled Access:	Yes. Toilet and parking for disabled on site. Wheelchairs on loan.
Tours/Events:	House tours and garden tours for groups by arrangement. Special evening tours with wine, music and canapes - contact for details.
Coach Parking:	Yes
Length of Visit:	4 hours
Booking Contact:	Elizabeth Blake Loseley Park, Estate Office, (Stakescorner Road), Guildford, Surrey, GU3 1HS Telephone: 01483 405112 Fax: 01483 302036 General Information: 01483 304440
Email:	enquiries@loseley-park.com **Website:** www.loseley-park.com
Location:	3 miles south of Guildford via A3 and B3000.

Please quote this guide when booking

Painshill Park is one of the most important 18th century parks in Europe. It is the artistic vision of one English gentleman, the Hon. Charles Hamilton, who created a series of subtle and surprising vistas between 1738 and 1773 – it was a pleasure ground for fashionable society. Now undergoing a unique and faithful restoration by a charitable Trust – Europa Nostra Medal winner for 'exemplary restoration'.

Within Painshill Park's 160 acres, The Hamilton Landscapes – which include Gothic Temple, Chinese Bridge, Crystal Grotto, 18th century plantings, Turkish Tent, Gothic Tower, newly restored Hermitage, working vineyard, giant Waterwheel feeding a 14-acre serpentine lake – are a work of art.

In Spring 2006, American Roots, a major horticultural exhibition, will open exploring the 18th century exchange of plants between Europe and America. The story of how American seeds changed European gardens forever.

Fact File

Opening Times: Open all year. (Closed Christmas Day and Boxing Day) March - October 2006: 10.30 a.m. – 6 p.m. or dusk (last entry 4.30 p.m.) November 2006 – February 2007: 10.30 a.m. – 4 p.m. or dusk (last entry 3 p.m.)

Admission Rates: Adults: £6.00. Senior Citizens: £5.25. Accompanied Children (5 – 16) £3.50, under 5's Free.

Group Rates: Minimum Groups Size: 10. £5.00pp. Guided Tour: £1 pp extra. Pre-booking essential.

Facilities: Visitor Centre. Shop. Tearoom.

Disabled Access: Yes. Toilet and car parking on site. Wheelchair Loan booking available.

Tours/Events: Guided tours available. Please call for details – events throughout the year

Coach Parking: Yes.

Length of Visit: 3 – 4 hours.

Booking Contact Sarah Hallett. Painshill Park Trust, Portsmouth Road, Cobham, Surrey KT11 1JE Telephone: 01932 868113 Fax: 01932 868001

Email: Info@painshill.co.uk **Website:** www.painshill.co.uk

Location: By road: Painshill Park can be reached via the M25 (J10) and the A3. Exit at junction with A245 towards Cobham. Entrance to free car park is in Between Streets, Cobham, (A245) 200m east of the A245/A307 roundabout. By Rail: from Waterloo to Cobham or Weybridge. Taxis available. By bus: Route 408 (Epsom Buses): Sutton/Leatherhead/Cobham (NOT SUNDAYS). Route 515 (Tellings Golden Miller): Kingston/Surbiton/Cobham/Wisley/Guildford.

Please quote this guide when booking

Ramster is famous for its stunning collection of rhododendrons and azaleas, which flourish under the mature woodland canopy. Established in the 1900s by Gauntlett Nurseries of Chiddingfold, with influences from the Japanese gardens, it now stretches over twenty acres.

April heralds the arrival of many varieties of daffodils, complementing the camellias, the early flowering rhododendrons and the stunning magnolias. The carpets of scented bluebells contrast exquisitely with the fiery display of azaleas and rhododendrons in May and the warmth of June brings forth the Mediterranean grasses, and the subtle pink climbing roses. In the bog garden a mass of colourful primulas cascade down the rill, and stepping-stones weave a path under the leaves of the giant gunnera.

Always peaceful and beautiful the changing colours are reflected in the pond and lake. Wildlife abounds throughout the season, including kingfishers, herons, ducks, geese and moorhens.

Fact File

Opening Times:	8th April – 25th June 2006: 10.00 a.m. – 5.00 p.m.
Admission Rates:	Adults: £4.00, Children: Under 16 – free.
Group Rates:	Minimum Groups Size: 15
	Adults: £4.00, Children: Under 16 – free.
Facilities:	Plant sales, homemade teas, light lunches and snacks.
Disabled Access:	Yes. Toilet and car parking on site.
Tours/Events:	Guided tours available. Open-air theatre 18th June – Romeo & Juliet.
Coach Parking:	Yes.
Length of Visit:	Between 30 minutes and 2 hours.
Booking Contact	Mrs. Elly Morgan
	Ramster Gardens, Petworth Road, Chiddingfold, Surrey GU8 4SN
	Telephone: 01428 642481/07817 105996 Fax: 01428 642481
Email:	info@ramsterweddings.co.uk
Website:	www.ramsterweddings.co.uk
Location:	1^1/2 miles south of Chiddingfold on the A283

Please quote this guide when booking

Titsey Place Gardens   Surrey

The Trustees are delighted to welcome visitors to Titsey Place and Gardens. The House which dates back to the 17th Century is home to four stunning Canaletto paintings, superb collection of porcelain and objets d'arts belonging to the Leveson Gower and Gresham families who have owned this beautiful mansion house in the North Downs. The gardens extend to some 15 acres and are a mix of formal lawns and rose gardens to informal walks around the two lakes. There is a modern Etruscan temple, walled kitchen garden and four miles of woodland walks. For further information visit www.titsey.org or telephone 01273 407056.

Fact File

Opening Times: 1 p.m. – 5 p.m. Mid-May to End September on Wednesdays and Sundays. Additionally open summer bank holidays. The garden only open on Easter Monday.

Admission Rates: Adults: £5.00, Senior Citizens: £5.00, Garden only: £2.50.

Group Rates: Please telephone for details
Adults/Senior Citizens/Children: £6.00

Facilities: Picnic Area.

Disabled Access: Yes, but garden only and not very easy. Toilet and parking on site.

Tours/Events: Guided tours of house & garden by arrangement.

Coach Parking: Yes. By arrangement only.

Length of Visit: 1 hour garden/ 45 minutes house.

Booking Contact Trish Humphrey-Smart
Titsey Place Gardens, Titsey Place, Oxted, Surrey RH8 0JD
Telephone: 01273 407017 Fax: 01273 478995

Email: trish.humphrey.smart@struttandparker.co.uk

Website: www.titsey.org

Location: From the A25 between Oxted & Westerham turn left onto B629 @ the end of Limpsfield High Street turn left & follow signs to visitors car park.

Please quote this guide when booking

With over 240 acres of garden there is plenty to see during your visit to RHS Garden Wisley. Its diversity and horticultural excellence providing visitors with ideas and inspiration all year round have made it one of the world's favourite gardens. Colour begins early in the year with witch hazels among the first to flower, followed by bulbs, blossom, new leaves and then the rhododendrons mean spring is always spectacular. Summer hits the garden in all areas with Mixed Borders, Roses and tropical plantings making a highlight. Autumn is no less colourful, with amazing yellows, oranges and reds on all kinds of plants, making way for the structure and design of the garden to become evident on the trees and shrubs in Seven Acres, Pinetum and Arboretum. Lastly other interesting areas include the Vegetable Garden, Fruit Garden and Orchard, Glasshouses, Trials Field and Rock Garden.

A visit is made complete by the Restaurant, Cafe, Coffee Shop, Orchard Cafe, the Shop with superb range of gifts and horticultural books plus the Plant Centre with over 10,000 plants for sale.

Fact File

Opening Times: All year except Christmas Day. Mon-Fri 10am - 6pm, Sat & Sun 9am - 6pm (4.30pm Nov - Feb). Bank Holidays 9am opening.

Admission Rates: Adults £7.50, Senior Citizen £7.50, Children £2.00 (6-16), under 6 free, RHS members. Carer/Companion of disabled Free.

Groups Rates: Minimum group size 10+ Adults £5.50, Children £1.60 (6-16), under 6 free.

Facilities: Cafe, Restaurant, Orchard Cafe, Coffee Shop, Plant Centre, Shop.

Disabled Access: Yes. Toilet and parking for disabled on site. Wheelchairs on loan, suggested route around garden.

Tours/Events: Guided tours Mon-Sat, £1.50 per person, group rate 10+ £1.00. Many events throughout the year, including flower shows, Apple Festival, and evening events.

Coach Parking: Yes, special coach park, coach driver refreshment voucher.

Length of Visit: 4 hours

Booking Contact: Sarah Martin, RHS Garden Wisley, Woking, Surrey, GU23 6QB Tel: 01483 212307 Fax: 01483 211750

Email: sarahmartin@rhs.org.uk

Website: www.rhs.org.uk

Location: In Surrey, on the A3 near to J10 of the M25.

Please quote this guide when booking

Gardens & Grounds of Herstmonceux Castle   East Sussex

Herstmonceux is renowned for its magnificent moated castle, set in beautiful parkland and superb Elizabethan Gardens. Built originally as a country home in the mid 15th century, Herstmonceux Castle embodies the history of medieval England and the romance of renaissance Europe. Set among carefully maintained Elizabethan Gardens and parkland, your experience begins with your first sight of the castle as it breaks into view.

In the grounds you will find the formal gardens including a walled garden dating from before 1570, a herb garden, the Shakespeare Garden, woodland sculptures, the Pyramid, the water lily filled moat and the Georgian style folly.

The Woodland walks will take you to the remains of three hundred year old sweet chestnut avenue, the rhododendron garden from the Lowther/Latham period, the waterfall (dependent on rainfall), and the 39 steps leading you through a woodland glade.

Fact File

Opening Times: 15th April - 29th October, open daily. **Closed 25th July.**

Admission Rates: Adults £4.95, Senior Citizen £3.95, Child £3.00 (5-15yrs).

Group Rates: Minimum group size: 15
Adults £3.95, Senior Citizen £3.50, Child/Students £2.00 (5-15yrs).

Facilities: Visitor Centre, Gift Shop, Tea Room, Nature Trail, Children's Woodland Play Area.

Disabled Access: Limited. Toilet and parking for disabled on site. 1 Wheelchair on loan. booking essential.

Tours/Events: Guided Tours are conducted at an extra charge and subject to availablity.
Please telephone for confirmation of tours before you visit.

Coach Parking: Yes

Length of Visit: 2 - 4 hours

Booking Contact: Caroline Dennett
Herstmonceux Castle, Hailsham, East Sussex, BN27 1RN
Telephone: 01323 834457 Fax: 01323 834499

Email: c_dennett@isc-queensu.ac.uk

Website: www.herstmonceux-castle.com

Location: Located just outside the village of Herstmonceux on the A271, entrance is on Wartling Road.

Please quote this guide when booking

King John's Garden & Nursery   East Sussex

This romantic garden extends to more than 5 acres with further acres of surrounding meadows with fine trees and grazing sheep. There are a number of water features including a lily pond and fountain in the formal garden which lies in front of the beautiful listed house. The wild garden and pond has a rustic bridge which leads you to the ivy garden.

The secret garden, a favourite area, and woodland walk brings visitors to the attractive garden house. A buttercup meadow takes you to the fine medieval barn covered in roses and white solanum. Sheep graze peacefully by joined by the many white fantail pigeons. Legend has it that King John II, who became King of France in 1350, was taken prisoner by the Black Prince and was held hostange in this house for some years before he died in 1364 in London. This house and garden is situated on the Kent/Sussex border (AONB) and has wonderful panoramic views. There are many special parts to this exceptional garden, including borders with softly-coloured roses and herbaceous plantings. A propagation nursery has now opened and is operated by the owners' son who has also become a dedicated gardener like his parents.

Fact File

Opening Times:	10.00 a.m. – 5 p.m. daily, not Christmas and New Year.
Admission Rates:	Adults: £3.50, Senior Citizens: £3.00, Children: £1.00 (over 6 years).
Group Rates:	Minimum Groups Size: 10
	Adults: £3.00, Senior Citizens: £2.50, Children: £0.50 (over 6 years)
Facilities:	Shop, plant sales, teas, lunch by arrangement, B&B and holiday accommodation.
Disabled Access:	Car parking on site and garden access.
Tours/Events:	Guided tours available.
Coach Parking:	Yes.
Length of Visit:	1 – 2 hours
Booking Contact	Jill & Richard Cunningham
	King John's Lodge, Sheepstreet Lane, Etchingham, East Sussex TN19 7AZ
	Telephone: 01580 819232 Fax: 01580 819562
Email:	kingjohnslodge@aol.com
Website:	www.kingjohnslodge.co.uk
Location:	West off the A21 at Hurst Green (265). At the end of Hurst Green village, turn right (Burgh Hill) then turn right again into Sheepstreet Lane. The house and garden is one mile on the left.

Please quote this guide when booking

Merriments Gardens East Sussex

A garden not be missed - **Merriments Garden** at **Hurst Green** offers everything for the "Garden Lover's" day out.

Set in 4 acres of gently sloping Weald farmland, this is a garden of richly and imaginatively planted deep curved borders, colour themed and planted in the great tradition of English gardening. These borders use a rich mix of trees, shrubs, perennials, grasses and many unusual annuals which ensure an arresting display of colour, freshness and vitality in the garden right through to its closing in autumn. Also in the garden are two large ponds, dry scree area, bog and wilder areas of garden planted only using plants suited for naturalising and colonising their environment. It delights all who visit.

The extensive Nursery offers a wide choice of unusual and interesting plants for sale many of which can be seen growing in the garden.

Fact File

Opening Times:	14th April to 30th September.
Admission Rates:	Adults £4.00, Senior Citizens £4.00, Child £2.00.
Group Rates:	Minimum group size: 12 (£3.50 per Adult)
Facilities:	Gift Shop, Plant Sales, Teas, Restaurant.
Disabled Access:	Yes. Toilet and parking for disabled on site, Wheelchairs on loan booking advisable.
Tours/Events:	None
Coach Parking:	Yes
Length of Visit:	2 - 3 hours
Booking Contact:	Alana Sharp
	Hawkhurst Road, Hurst Green, East Sussex. TN19 7RA.
	Telephone: 01580 860666 Fax: 01580 860324
Email:	info@merriments.co,uk
Website:	www.merriments.co.uk
Location:	15 miles north of Hastings just off the A21 at Hurst Green.

Please quote this guide when booking

Michelham Priory & Gardens

East Sussex

Boasting England's longest water-filled medieval moat encircling seven acres of beautiful grounds and gardens, discover nearly 800 years of history at Michelham Priory.

On this peaceful "island of history" explore the impressive 14th century gatehouse, working watermill and magnificent (reputedly haunted) Tudor Mansion that evolved from the former Augustinian Priory. In the grounds ingenious planting of the landscaped gardens offers the visitor an ever-changing display of beauty, whatever the season, while the physic, cloister, and kitchen gardens add extra interest. Recently featured in Country Life and The English Garden, the gardens at Michelham leave a positive and lasting impression on all who visit them.

Fact File

Opening Times: 1st March - 31st Oct, Tuesday - Sunday from 10.30am
Also open daily in August and on Bank Holidays.
Closing times, March and October 4.30pm, April - July and September 5pm, August 5.30pm.

Admission Rates: Adults £5.60, Senior Citizen & Student £4.70, Child £2.90, Disabled/Carer £2.80 each, Family (2 + 2) £14.30

Groups Rates: Minimum group size: 15
Adults £4.50, Senior Citizen & Student £4.50, Child £2.60
Free admission for coach drivers and tourist guides on production of a 'blue badge'

Facilities: Shop, Restaurant, Cafe, Plant Sales.

Disabled Access: Yes. Toilet and parking for disabled on site. Loan wheelchairs available, booking advised.

Tours/Events: Guided tours organised for groups on request. Spring Garden Festival 8 - 9 April.

Coach Parking: Yes. Free refreshments for coach drivers.

Length of Visit: 3 - 4 hours

Booking Contact: Frances Preedy. Michelham Priory, Upper Dicker, Nr Hailsham, East Sussex, BN27 3QS
Telephone: 01323 844224   Fax: 01323 844030

Email: adminmich@sussexpast.co.uk   **Website:** www.sussexpast.co.uk

Location: 2 miles west of Hailsham & 8 miles north west of Eastbourne. Signposted from A22 & A27. (OS map 198 TQ558 093).

Please quote this guide when booking

Pashley Manor Gardens

East Sussex

The de Passele family built a moated Manor in 1262 and held the estate untill 1453, when it was sold to the forebears of Anne Boleyn. It is possible that Anne, second wife of Henry VIII, stayed here during her childhood. In 1543 the estate was sold to Sir Thomas May, who built the Tudor house you see today, the fine Georgian Facade was added in 1720.

The Gardens offer a sumptuous blend of romantic landscaping, imaginative plantings and fine old trees, fountains, springs and large ponds. This is a quintessential English Garden of a very individual character, with exceptional views to the surrounding valleyed fields. Many eras of English history are reflected here, typlfylng the tradltlon of the English Country House and its Garden.

Pashley now holds a Tulip Festival in May, Spring and Summer Plant Fairs, Special Summer Rose weekend, open air Opera, The Sussex Guild Craft Show and an exhibition of Sculptures and botanical art lasting throughout the season.

Fact File

Opening Times:	8th April - 30th September, Tuesday, Wednesday, Thursday & Saturday 11am - 5pm.
Admission Rates:	(2005 Rates) Adults £6.00, Senior Citizen £6.00, Child £5.50.
Groups Rates:	Minimum group size 20 Adults £5.50, Senior Citizen £5.50.
Facilities:	Shop, Plant Sales, Teas, Licensed Cafe, Light Lunches.
Disabled Access:	Limited. Toilet and parking for disabled on site. Wheelchairs on loan, Booking necessary.
Tours/Events:	Tours of garden available. Please call for special event details.
Coach Parking:	Yes
Length of Visit:	2 1/2 hours
Booking Contact:	Claire Baker Pashley Manor Gardens, Ticehurst, East Sussex, TN5 7HE Tel: 01580 200888 Fax: 01580 200102
Email:	info@pashleymanorgardens.com
Website:	www.pashleymanorgardens.com
Location:	On the B2099 between the A21 and Ticehurst village (Tourist brown-signed).

Please quote this guide when booking

Borde Hill Garden, Park & Woodland   West Sussex

Winner of the HHA/Christies 'Garden of the Year' 2004, this glorious heritage Grade II* listed Garden offers beauty for all seasons. Heralded by magnificent magnolias, rhododendrons and azaleas, spring blends into summer with fragrant roses and herbaceous plants. In the autumn visitors enjoy rich colour and in the winter architectural splendour with the Victorian glasshouses offering warmth and interest.

A plantsman's paradise with 'Champion' trees complementing rare shrubs introduced by the great plant collectors over 100 years ago. This unique collection of trees extends to many woodland gardens and includes native hardwoods and specimen trees.

Enjoy the distinctive formal 'garden rooms', including the sumptuous Rose Garden and the romantic Italian Garden. Find peace and tranquillity in the informal Azalea Ring and the Garden of Allah, and drama in the sub-tropical Round Dell. Set in 200 acres of parkland, the Garden affords panoramic views across the Ouse Valley and towards the South Downs. Lakeside walks to explore and picnic.

Fact File

Opening Times:	See our website or ring for opening times.
Admission Rates:	Mid March - Mid October - Adults £6.00, Senior Citizen £5.00, Child £3.50.
	Mid October - End Dec - Adults £4.00, Senior Citizen £4.00, Child £2.50.
	No concessions during May and June.
Group Rates:	Minimum group size: 20 +
	Mid March - Mid October - Adults £5.00, Senior Citizen £5.00, Child £3.00.
Facilities:	Gift Shop, Tearooms, Jeremy's Restaurant (Good Food Guide 2006), Coarse Fishing, Adventure playground, Dogs on Leads Welcome.
Disabled Access:	Yes, Toilet and parking for disabled on site. Wheelchairs on loan, booking advisable.
Tours/Events:	Special events programme throughout the year.
Coach Parking:	Yes.
Length of Visit:	2 - 4 hours
Booking Contact:	The Administrator, Borde Hill Garden, Balcombe Road, Haywards Heath West Sussex, RH16 1XP. Telephone: 01444 450326 Fax: 01444 440427
Email:	debbie@bordehill.co.uk
Website:	www.bordehill.co.uk
Location:	From London, Junction 10a on A23, From Brighton 20 mins by road, 1 1/2 miles north of Haywards Heath railway station.

Please quote this guide when booking

A beautiful garden designed for year-round interest – through use of form, colour and texture. Nearly 4 acres in size and the home of John Brookes MBE, renowned garden designer and writer, it is a garden full of ideas to be interpreted within smaller home spaces.

Gravel is used extensively in the garden both to walk on and as a growing medium so that you walk through the plantings rather than past them. A dry gravel 'stream' meanders down to a large natural looking pond. There is a walled garden, conservatory and a glass area for tender plants.

There is a fully licensed Garden Café (Les Routiers Café of the Year 2005 for London & East) which serves a selection of light lunches, coffees, teas and a variety of delicious cakes and a beautiful Plant Centre which stocks around 1500 varieties of perennials and shrubs.

Fact File

Opening Times:	Daily all year round 9am - 5pm. (Except 25th, 26th Dec & 1st Jan)
Admission Rates:	Adults £3.95, Senior Citizens £3.45, Child (4-16 years) £2.25.
Group Rates:	Minimum group size: 15
	Adults 3.25, Senior Citizens £3.25.
Facilities:	Plant Centre, Cafe, Gift Shop.
Disabled Access:	Yes, Wheelchairs on loan, booking advisable.
Tours/Events:	Guided Tours.
Coach Parking:	Yes.
Length of Visit:	2 - 3 hours
Booking Contact:	Claudia Murphy,
	Denmans Garden, Denmans Lane, Fontwell, West Sussex BN18 0SU.
	Telephone: 01243 542 808 Fax: 01243 544 064
Email:	denmans@denmans-garden.co.uk
Website:	www.denmans-garden.co.uk
Location:	Situated off A27 (westbound) between Chichester 6 mls and Arundel 5 mls adjacent to Fontwell Racecourse. The nearest railway station in Barnham 3 mls.

Please quote this guide when booking

High Beeches Woodland & Water Gardens   Sussex

Discover twenty five acres of magically beautiful, peaceful, woodland and water gardens. Wander through enchanting vistas, down winding paths, through open sunlit glades, by still pools and rippling waterfalls. Especially colourful in spring and autumn, High Beeches is a romantic landscape, changing with the seasons, and remote from the stresses of modern life.

In spring see sheets of daffodils, followed by bluebells, in the woodland glades. Later, the magnolias and azaleas are at their best, and in summer the natural Wildflower Meadows are full of wild orchids, cowslips, and many other flowers. Seek out the many rare plants, including the National Collection of Stewartia Trees, and follow our Tree Trail.

In August, the wonderful azure blue Willow Gentians are in bloom throughout the gardens, and in Autumn, the scene alters again, as the varied foliage changes to a splendid crescendo of crimson, copper, and gold.

Fact File

Opening Times:	13.00 hours – 17.00 hours, last admission 16.30 hours.
Admission Rates:	Adults/Senior Citizens: £5.50, Children: Under 14 Free.
Group Rates:	£4.50 for groups over 30 in number
Facilities:	Visitor Centre, Plant Sales, Restaurant, Teas.
Disabled Access:	Yes, partial. Toilet and parking on site.
Tours/Events:	Guided tours available.
Coach Parking:	Yes.
Length of Visit:	1 1/2 - 2 hours.
Booking Contact	Sarah Bray. High Beeches Woodland and Water Gardens, Handcross, Haywards Heath, Sussex RH17 6HQ Telephone: 01444 400589 Fax: 01444 401543
Email:	gardens@highbeeches.com
Website:	www.highbeeches.com
Location:	1 mile east of the A23 at Handcross on the south side of the B2110 in mid-Sussex.

In Spring, the sumptuous blooms of azaleas and rhododendrons (some 200 years old) overhang paths lined with bluebells in this romantic 240-acre valley with walks around seven lakes. Watch the wildfowl and glimpse the deer and wallabies.

Enjoy the glorious rock Garden, admire the art of beautiful Bonsai, and marvel at the collection of Victorian Motorcars (1889 - 1900).

Visit the extended 'Behind the Doll's house" exhibition. This shows a country estate and local market town of 100 years ago - all in miniature 1/12th scale.

The Clock Tower Restaurant for morning coffee, lunches and teas. There is a Gift Shop and a wide selection of Plants for sale.

Fact File

Opening Times: 1st April - 31st October 9.30am - 6pm

Admission Rates: May (Saturdays, Sundays) £9.00, May (Monday - Friday) £8.00, April & June to October £6.00, Children aged 5-15yrs - (Anytime) £4.00

Groups Rates: Minimum group size: 20
May (Saturdays, Sundays) £8.00, May (Monday - Friday) £7.00,
April & June to October £5.00, Children aged 5-15yrs - (Anytime) £3.50

Facilities: Shop, Restaurant, Plant Sales.

Disabled Access: No

Tours/Events: 29th April - 1st May, Bonsai Weekend & demonstrations. 15th - 16th July; Model Boat Regatta.

Coach Parking: Yes (Free)

Length of Visit: 4 - 5 hours

Booking Contact: Thomas Loder. Leonardslee Gardens, Lower Beeding, Horsham, West Sussex, RH13 6PP
Telephone: 01403 891212   Fax: 01403 891305

Email: gardens@leonardslee.com

Website: www.leonardslee.com

Location: 4 miles from Handcross at bottom of M23 via B2110, entrance is at junction of B2110 and A281, between Handcross and Cowfold.

Please quote this guide when booking

142

Parham House & Gardens   West Sussex

Nestling at the base of the South Downs, Parham Park is a beautiful Elizabethan House. A herd of black fallow deer, established here for over 400 years, graze the surrounding medieval deer park. From the House visitors find themselves in the Pleasure Grounds where flowing lawns lead to the Lake with vistas into the surrounding parklands and the Downs beyond.

The walled garden, itself the subject of major articles in the Country's leading horticultural magazines, contains herbaceous and mixed borders, vibrant in colour and opulent in style. Designed to excite for a long season, peaking in summer and late autumn, the textures of the borders echo the precious tapestries in the House.

Parham is justly famous for the long tradition of informal flower arrangements that decorate the House throughout the season, all of which are supplied from the Gardens where there are huge borders and beds and an almost kaleidoscopic sea of colour.

Fact File

Opening Times: Easter Sunday - end of September. Wednesdays, Thursdays, Sundays and Bank Holiday Mondays (August additional Tuesdays and Fridays).
Gardens open, 12pm , House open - 2pm - 5pm (last entry).

Admission Rates: Gardens only: Adult £5.00 (exc. Gift Aid), Senior Citizen/Disabled/Carer £4.50.
House & Gardens: Adult £6.80 (exc. Gift Aid), Senior Citizen/Disabled/Carer £6.00.

Group Rates: Discounted rates for group advanced bookings.

Facilities: Restaurant selling light lunches from 12 noon and teas from 2.30pm, Gift Shop, Picnic Area, Plant Sales, Shop, Brick & Turf Maze, Wendy House.

Disabled Access: Yes. Toilet and parking for disabled on site.

Tours/Events: Parham Garden Weekend, 8th - 9th July 2006, (Special admission rates).

Coach Parking: Yes. No Charge.

Length of Visit: 2 - 3 hours

Booking Contact: Feona Clarke, Parham House & Gardens, Storrington, Pulborough, West Sussex, RH20 4HS. Telephone: 01903 742021 Fax: 01903 746557.

Email: bookings@parhaminsussex.co.uk

Website: www.parhaminsussex.co.uk

Location: Parham is located on the A283 midway between Storrington and Pulborough, Equidistant from the A24 or A29.

Please quote this guide when booking

From the small gravel garden with clipped box and yew, the path leads over a pretty stone balustraded bridge to the topiary garden in front of the fifteenth-century timber-framed house. The yew tunnel beyond the gate leads to the ivy-clad Monk's Walk. The top lawn is enclosed by herbaceous beds, while the lower lawn has clipped yew hedges and roses, with a beautiful *Ginkgo Biloba*, and lower down a small pond.

The Victorian 'Secret' Garden boasts a 40-metre fruit wall with the original heated pineapple pits and stove house, the Jubilee Rose Garden in memory of the late Queen Mother, herbaceous borders and yew hedges. The Terracotta garden has been planted with box, giving structure to the planned herb garden. The circular orchard is being restored, and a woodland walk created, with underplanting of bluebells and primroses. The original Boulton and Paul potting shed houses a rural museum.

"One of Britain's Fifty Best Gardens to Visit" (The Independent)

Fact File

Opening Times:	May to end of September (House and Gardens). Public open afternoons Suns, Thurs, BH Mondays 2-6pm (last entry 5pm). Groups at other times by appointment.
Admission Rates:	Adults £6.00, Senior Citizen £5.00, Child £2.50.
Group Rates:	Groups (of 25 or more). Adults £5.50, Child £2.50.
Facilities:	Gift Shop, Teas, Car Park.
Disabled Access:	Partial.
Tours/Events:	Guided tours of House and Gardens.
Coach Parking:	Yes.
Length of Visit:	2 hours.
Booking Contact:	Jean Whitaker St Mary's House, Bramber, West Sussex, BN44 3WE. Tel: 01903 816205 Fax: 01903 816205
Email:	info@stmarysbramber.co.uk
Website:	www.stmarysbramber.co.uk
Location:	8 miles NE of worthing off A283 in Bramber, 1 mile east of Steyning.

Please quote this guide when booking

West Dean Gardens

A place of tranquility and beauty in the rolling South Downs all year round, West Dean features a restored walled kitchen garden with some of the finest Victorian glasshouses in the country. Over 200 varieties of carefully trained fruit trees, rows of vegetables and an array of exotic flowers and produce are produced in the walled garden. Visit rustic summerhouses, a 300ft Edwardian pergola, ornamental borders and a pond in the extensive grounds. A circular walk through the 49-acre arboretum offers breathtaking views of the surrounding countryside and the fine flint mansion of West Dean College in its parkland setting. The visitor centre has a licensed restaurant and gift shop. Garden events take place throughout the summer.

Fact File

Opening Times: Open daily May - September 10.30am - 5pm. March - April & October 11am - 5pm. November to February 11am - 4.30pm (Wednesday to Sunday only).

Admission Rates: Adults £6.00, Over 60's £5.00, Child £2.00.

Group Rates: Minimum group size: 20
Adults £5.00, Over 60's £5.00, Child £2.00.

Facilities: Visitor Centre, Shop, Plant Sales, Teas, Restaurant.

Disabled Access: Limited. Toilet and parking for disabled on site. Wheelchairs on loan, booking necessary.

Tours/Events: Tours by appointment only.
Annual events programme, please enquire for details.

Coach Parking: Yes.

Length of Visit: 2 - 4 hours.

Booking Contact: Celia Dickinson
West Dean Gardens, West Dean, Chichester, West Sussex, PO18 0QZ.
Tel: 01243 818210 Fax: 01243 811301

Email: gardens@westdean.org.uk

Website: www.westdean.org.uk

Location: On A286 6 miles north of Chichester.

Please quote this guide when booking

Created over the last decade the gardens are mature and varied. Visitors can enjoy the delights within the different areas: The Courtyard with Elizabethan Knot Garden, The Walled Garden, The Courtyard, The Bog Garden, Riverside and Lake Walks amongst others.

Opened in 1996 the Walled Garden is a splendid example of individual 'garden rooms' one of the most spectacular is the Rose Labyrinth, celebrated during the annual Rose Festival in June when it becomes rich with colour and perfume. There are beautiful 'hot' and 'cold' herbaceous borders containing plants, nurtured at Coughton Court, which are also on sale to visitors.

Thanks to the enthusiasm of the Throckmorton family, the gardens are now considered to be some of the finest in the country. In fact, the gardens have now become as big a draw as the house itself.

Fact File

Opening Times: Please call our info line on 01789 762435 or visit our website www.coughtoncourt.co.uk for details.

Admission Rates: Please call to confirm 2006 admission prices or visit our website.

Group Rates: Minimum group size: 15 (paying visitors) House & Gardens: £7.50, Gardens only: £5.15

Facilities: Shop, Plant Sales, Teas, Restaurant, Gunpowder Plot Exhibition.

Disabled Access: Yes (Gardens only), Toilet and parking for disabled on site.

Tours/Events: There is a programme of events from April to Christmas

Parking: All Cars £1.00. Coaches by prior arrangement.

Length of Visit: 3 hours

Booking Contact: Coughton Court, Alcester, Warwickshire, B49 5JA. Telephone: 01789 400777 Fax: 01789 765544

Email: sales@throckmortons.co.uk

Website: www.coughtoncourt.co.uk

Location: Take the A435 from Alcester towards Birmingham, the House is signposted from the road.

Please quote this guide when booking

Ragley Hall & Gardens   Warwickshire

The bare bones of Robert Marnock's late 19th century garden carved from Lancelot Brown's sculptured parkland remains in evidence today around this splendid Palladian Hall. However, unlike Marnock's original vision intended to show off discoveries from the New World, the ethos now focuses on indigenous flora and fauna. Marnock's garden has matured into a rich palette for nature with mature trees predominating throughout producing a magnificent foil for new developments. A naturalistic and less contrived approach has sought to create and optimise natural habitat, increasing biodiversity, without compromising the garden's aesthetic appeal. The result is a garden in which traditional horticultural features such as the Rose Garden, herbaceous borders and formal bedding blend effortlessly with areas of wild flower meadow and a wildlife pond. Ragley Hall also boasts the prestigious Jerwood Sculpture Collection and the gardens provide a unique backdrop for many thought-provoking pieces.

Fact File

Opening Times: 25th March - 1st October, Thurs - Sun + Bank Holiday Mondays. Open daily during School Holidays. Saturday and Sunday in October.

Admission Rates: Adults £6.00, Senior Citizen £5.50, Child £4.50
House included - Adults £7.50, Senior Citizen £6.50, Child £4.50. (Thursday to Sunday)

Group Rates: 20
Adults £5.00, Senior Citizen £5.00, Child £3.00
House included - Adults £6.00, Senior Citizen £6.00, Child £3.00.

Facilities: Gift Shop, Plant Sales, Teas, Hooke's Coffee House & Restaurant, Adventure Playground, Lakeside Picnic & Play Area, Jerwood Sculpture Park, Woodland Walks.

Disabled Access: Yes. Toilet and parking for disabled on site. Wheelchairs on loan. Booking advisable.

Tours/Events: Various events please call for details, and visit www.ragleyhall.com.

Coach Parking: Yes

Length of Visit: 2 + hours

Booking Contact: Michelle Malin, Ragley Hall, Alcester, Warwickshire, B49 5NJ
Telephone: 01789 762090 ext 125   Fax: 01789 764791

Email: Info@ragleyhall.com

Website: www. ragleyhall.com

Location: Ragley lies 8 miles West of Stratford-Upon-Avon, 2 miles From Alcester off the A46/A435.

Please quote this guide when booking

The Shakespeare Gardens contain many of the plants and herbs mentioned in Shakespeare's writing and are immaculately maintained by a dedicated team of gardeners. Each garden has its own unique character and reflects traditional gardening styles and practices from 16th Century to the present day. Features include the, Cottage Garden, Orchard, Sculpture Garden, Maze, History of Gardening exhibition and Romantic Willow Cabin at Anne Hathaway's Cottage, Elizabethan style Knot Garden and historic Great Garden at Nash's House & New Place and Herbal Bed and Ancient Mulburry Tree at Hall's Croft.

The gardens have been enjoyed by visitors to the Shakespeare Houses for over a century. Now, the Shakespeare Birthplace Trust is offering an escorted 'gardens only' tour of the grounds of Anne Hathaway's Cottage, Nash's House & New Place and Hall's Croft. The tour will last approximately three hours and will be led by the Trust's Head Gardener or a senior member of his team.

Fact File

Opening Times:	Easter to September 2005.
Admission Rates:	Adults £9.00, Senior Citizen £7.50, Child £4.50.
	NB, Rates are for a tour of all three gardens and do not include admission in to the Shakespeare Houses.
Group Rates:	Minimum group size: 10
Facilities:	Gift Shop, Tea Room.
Disabled Access:	Partial. Toilet and parking for disabled on site, Wheelchairs on loan at Anne Hathaway's Cottage only. Booking Advisable.
Tours/Events:	Guided garden tours available.
Coach Parking:	Yes. Anne Hathaway's Cottage.
Length of Visit:	2 - 3 hours.
Booking Contact:	(Group Visits Office)
	Shakespeare Birthplace Trust, Henley Street, Stratford-Upon-Avon, CV37 6QW
	Tel: 01789 201806/201836 Fax: 01789 263138
Email:	groups@shakespeare.org.uk
Website:	www.shakespeare.org.uk
Location:	Tours start at Anne Hathaway's Cottage, Shottery (1 mile from Stratford-Upon-Avon).

Please quote this guide when booking

Abbey House Gardens   Wiltshire

Now attracting groups from around the world, Alan Titchmarsh was right to say "The WOW! Factor is here in abundance!.

Britain's largest collection of roses flower throughout summer and autumn, after 100,000 tulips and thousands of narcissi and hyacinth in spring plus camellias, rhododendrons, meconopsis. A huge iris collection, laburnum tunnel, gorgeous wisteria and clematis, herbaceous borders rivalling Monet's, alstroemerias, lilies and Japanese maples; in fact a collection of plants bigger than some Botanic Gardens. And then, there's the unique herb garden with cloistered fruit walk; wooded walks to the river, monastic fish ponds and waterfall; all adjoining the ancient Benedictine Abbey church of Malmesbury, within the mediaeval hilltop town with shops, restaurants and pubs. No wonder groups are voting to visit us again and again and at different seasons. Don't let your group miss out on this wonderful experience.

Fact File

Opening Times: 11am - 5.30pm 21st March - 21st October.
Admission Rates: Adults £5.50, Concessions £5.00, Child £2.00
Groups Rates: Minimum group size 20. £4.75 per person.
Facilities: Plant Sales, Teas.
Disabled Access: Yes.
Tours/Events: 10th Anniversary events; Plays, Demonstrations, Sculpture and Exhibitions.
See website for additional information.
Coach Parking: Yes
Length of Visit: 2 hours minimum
Booking Contact: Geraldine Wilkins. Abbey House Gardens, Market Cross, Malmesbury, Wiltshire, SN16 9AS
Telephone: 01666 827650   Fax: 01666 822782
Email: info@abbeyhousegardens.co.uk
Website: www.abbeyhousegardens.co.uk
Location: In Malmesbury town centre. Off A429 between M4 junction 17 (5 miles) and Cirencester (12 miles). Coaches drop passengers in centre of town, 3 minute level walk from garden. Cars follow signs for long-stay car park from Malmesbury town centre. Garden is 5 min walk across the bridge, up the Abbey steps and entered left of Cloister Garden.

Please quote this guide when booking

Broadleas is a 10 acre garden on green sand soil which allows acid loving plants to thrive. Mature and semi-mature magnolias grow on each side of a steep dell. As good as any Cornish garden, it is full of fine things normally considered too tender for these parts. There are large specimens of everything (much of it now 50 years old) - Paulownia Fargesii, Parrotia Persica, all manner of magnolias, azaleas, hydrangeas hostas, lilies and trilliums of rare and notable species. It is a garden of tireless perfectionism, at its most stunning in spring when sheets of bulbs stretch out beneath the flowering trees. There is also a Perennial Garden, Sunken Rose Garden and Grey Border with a great variety of shrubs and exotic climbers and a Woodland Walk where a few tender rarities are hidden away for protection from the elements.

Fact File

Opening Times:	April - October 2 - 6pm , Sunday, Wednesday, Thursday.
Admission Rates:	April - October, Adults £5.00, Children under 10 £1.50.
Groups Rates:	Minimum group size 10 - £4.50
Facilities:	Teas for tours only by arrangement, Plant Sales
Disabled Access:	Partial.
Tours/Events:	Coach Tours
Coach Parking:	Yes
Length of Visit:	1 1/2 Hours
Booking Contact:	Lady Anne Cowdray
	Broadleas Gardens, Broadleas, Devizes, Wilts, SN10 5JQ
	Telephone: 01380 722035
Email:	broadleasgardens@btinternet.com
Website:	None
Location:	1 1/2 miles from centre of Devizes on A360 Salisbury Road..

Please quote this guide when booking

Heale House Garden & Plant Centre   Wiltshire

Heale House and its eight acres of beautiful garden, lie beside the river Avon, at Middle Woodford, just north of Salisbury. Much of the house is unchanged since King Charles II hid here in 1651.

In January great drifts of snowdrops and aconites bring early colour and this promise of spring is followed by magnificent magnolias and acers that surround the authentic Japanese Tea House and red Niko Bridge. The garden provides wonderfully varied collection of plants, shrubs, musk and other roses, a working kitchen garden, all growing in the formal setting of clipped hedges and mellow stonework and particularly lovely in June and July,. As summer turns to Autumn, Cyclamen, Nerines and Viburnums are in flower and trees and shrubs in the Japanese Garden display their brilliant autumnal foliage before leaf fall and the start of winter flowering shrubs and Hellebores.

Fact File

Opening Times: Garden: Tuesday - Sunday 10am - 5pm (open Bank Holiday Mondays) all year.
Plant Centre: Monday - Sunday 10am - 5pm all year.

Admission Rates: Adults £4.00, Senior Citizen £4.00, Child £1.50 (5-15yrs)

Groups Rates: Minimum group size: 20
Adults £3.75, Senior Citizen £3.75, Child £1.50 (5-15yrs)

Facilities: Shop, Plant Sales, Light lunches and refreshments Weds - Sun.

Disabled Access: Yes.

Tours/Events: Snowdrop weekends, 5th and 12th February. Guided tour and hot food on these first Sunday's in February of the Snowdrop and Winter Aconite display.

Coach Parking: Yes

Length of Visit: 1 1/2 - 2 hours

Booking Contact: David or Jill Holme.
Heale House, Middle Woodford, Nr Salisbury, Wiltshire, SP4 6NT
Telephone: 01722 782504   Fax: 01722 782504

Email: None

Website: None

Location: Four miles from Salisbury, Wilton and Stonehenge, on the 'Woodford Valley' road between the A360 and A345.

Please quote this guide when booking

The splendour of Longleat House nestling alongside a lake and within rolling 'Capability' Brown landscaped grounds is a view that cannot be missed. Fringed by thousands of trees the grounds include formal gardens, a 'Secret Garden' the 'Pleasure Walk', a 19th century planting of Rhododendrons and azaleas, topiary and fine examples of mazes including the Love Labyrinth, the Sun Maze and the Lunar Labyrinth.

A recent addition to Longleat are standing stones at Heaven's Gate - the massive stones and a ring-shaped 'gateway' - made up of 13 smaller stones - form part of a gigantic sculpture which was commissioned by the Seventh Marquess of Bath.

Fact File

Opening Times:	Open Daily, (except Christmas Day) Easter to September 10am - 5.30pm, Guided tours available 10am to 11am. Rest of year guided tours at set times between 11am and 3pm, may be subject to change.
Admission Rates:	Please Telephone for details.
Groups Rates:	Minimum group size: 12 Please telephone for details.
Facilities:	Shops, Restaurant and Cafe.
Disabled Access:	Yes. Toilet and parking for disabled on site. Wheelchairs on loan, booking necessary.
Tours/Events:	See website for our specialist garden tours or telephone for details.
Coach Parking:	Yes
Length of Visit:	A Full Day
Booking Contact:	Scott Sims Longleat, Warminster, Wiltshire, BA12 7NW Telephone : 01985 844328 Fax: 01985 844763
Email:	enquiries@longleat.co.uk
Website:	www.longleat.co.uk
Location:	Longleat is situated just off the A36 between Bath and Salisbury (A362 Warminster - Frome).

Please quote this guide when booking

The Peto Garden   Wiltshire

Romantically sited overlooking the valley of the River Frome, close to Badford-on-Avon, Iford Manor is built into the hillside below a hanging beechwood and fine garden terraces. The house was owned during the first part of the last century by Harold Peto, the architect and landscape designer who taught Lutyens, and who expressed his passion for classical Italian architecture and landscaping in an English setting, After many visits to Italy he acquired statues and architectural marbles. He planted phillyrea and cypress trees and other Mediterranean species to add to the plantings of the eighteenth century and to enhance the Italian character of the garden.

The great terrace is bounded on one side by an elegant colonnade and commands lovely views out over the orchard and the surrounding countryside. Paths wander through the Woodland and garden to the summerhouse, the cloister and the casita and amongst the water features.

Fact File

Opening Times:	2pm - 5pm Sundays April and October. 2pm - 5pm Tuesdays - Thursdays, Saturday, Sunday and Bank Holiday Mondays, May to September, Mornings and Mondays and Fridays reserved for group visits by Appointment.
Admission Rates:	Adults £4.50, Senior Citizen £4.00, Child over 10 yrs £4.00.
Group Rates:	Miimum group size: 8 Adults £5.00, Senior Citizen £5.00, Child over 10 yrs £5.00
Facilities:	House Keeper Teas - May to August at weekends
Disabled Access:	Yes, Toilet and parking for disabled on site.
Tours/Events:	By appointment
Coach Parking:	Yes.
Length of Visit:	1 1/2 hours
Booking Contact:	Mrs Elizabeth Cartwright-Hignett The Peto Garden, Iford Manor, Bradford on Avon, Wiltshire BA15 2BA Telephone:01225 863146 Fax: 01225 862364
Website:	www.ifordmanor.co.uk
Location:	Follow brown tourist signs to Iford Manor. 7 miles south of Bath on A36 Warminster Road and 1/2 mile south of Bradford on Avon on B3109.

Please quote this guide when booking

An outstanding example of the English landscape style, this splendid garden was designed by Henry Hoare II and laid out between 1741 and 1780. Classical temples, including the Pantheon and the Temple of Apollo, are situated around the central lake at the end of a series of vistas, which change as the visitor moves around the paths and through the magnificent mature woodland with its extensive collection of trees and shrubs.

Although Stourhead has changed and developed over more than two centuries, it remains as Horace Walpole described it in the 18th century: "One of the most picturesque scenes in the world".

The Stourhead Estate extends from the edge of the Wiltshire Downs in the east to King Alfred's Tower in the west, a 160 ft folly with views across Somerset, Dorset and Wiltshire.

Fact File

Opening Times: All year, daily from 9am until 7pm, or dusk if earlier.
(House open Friday - Tuesday, 18th March - 31st October 11.30am - 4.30pm).

Admission Rates: Adults £6.20, Child £3.40, National Trust Members free.

Group Rates: Minimum group size: 15, Adults £5.40, National Trust Members free.

Facilities: Visitor Centre, Shop, Plant Sales, Self Service Restaurant, Spread Eagle Inn.

Disabled Access: Yes. Toilet and parking for disabled on site. Wheelchairs on loan.

Tours/Events: Many different group packages available including lunch or refreshments. Contemporary Sculpture exhibition in September and October. Please ask for the Group information Guide. Walks, talks, painting, music, theatre & childrens events take all year. For events leaflet call 01747 841152

Coach Parking: Yes.

Length of Visit: Minimum 2 hours.

Booking Contact: Georgina Mead. Stourhead Estate Office, Stourton, Nr Mere, Warminster, Wiltshire BA12 6QD
Tel: 01747 841152 Fax: 01747 842005

Email: stourhead@nationaltrust.org.uk

Website: www.nationaltrust.org.uk

Location: Stourhead is in the village of Stourton, off the B3092, 3 miles north west of Mere (A303). It is 8 miles south of Frome (A361).

The gardens at Wilton House have changed considerably over the years, often reflecting the styles of the day and the individual tastes of each Earl and Countess of Pembroke. In an idyllic setting the grounds are bordered by the rivers Wylye and Nadder. A mix of open parkland in the style of 'Capability Brown' and small formal gardens. The latter created by the 17th Earl who began a programme of garden development soon after succeeding to the title in 1969.

The four new gardens created are the Rose Garden, the Water Garden, the Tudor Knot Garden and the North Forecourt Garden. There are a wealth of architectural features from the earlier Renaissance and 18th century gardens. There is also a woodland walk with its collection of many interesting trees from around the world. The latest addition of the Millennium Water Feature forms a contrast to the famous Palladian Bridge.

Fact File

Opening Times: 13th April - 30th September 2006.
Admission Rates: House & Grounds (Grounds Only) Adults £9.75 (£4.50), Senior Citizen £8.00 (£4.50), Child £5.50 (£3.50).
Group Rates: Minimum group size: 15
Adults £7.00, Senior Citizen £6.50, Child £4.50.
Facilities: Visitor Centre, Gift Shop, Teas, Historic House and Exhibitions. Plant Sales at adjacent Garden Centre.
Disabled Access: Yes. Toilet and parking for disabled on site. Wheelchairs on loan, booking advisable.
Tours/Events: Events Programme. See website.
Coach Parking: Yes.
Length of Visit: 4 1/2 hours - House & Grounds. 3 hours - Grounds only.
Booking Contact: Wilton House, Wilton, Salisbury, Wiltshire, SP2 0BJ
Tel: 01722 746720 Fax: 01722 744447
Email: tourism@wiltonhouse.com
Website: www.wiltonhouse.com
Location: 3 miles west of Salisbury off the A36

Please quote this guide when booking

Arley Arboretum & Gardens   Worcestershire

This jewel in Worcestershire's crown was, until four years ago, opened only occasionally to the public and is possibly the oldest privately owned Arboretum in the country. It is a haven of peace and tranquillity which overlooks the banks of the River Severn close to the picturesque village of Upper Arley. Approached through rolling parkland, entrance is made through a listed Walled Garden which contains an Italianate Garden, raised beds, orchard, Herbaceous borders, ornamental fowl, picnic area and plant sales.

With planting commencing in 1820 by Lord Mountnorris, it is now a mature and majestic Arboretum with awe-inspiring trees (some of which are record breaking and includes the tallest Crimean Pine in Britain) underplanted with rhododendrons, azaleas and camellias and 1000's of spring flowering bulbs together with a delightful Magnolia Walk.

Fact File

Opening Times: 1st April - 31st October.
Wednesday, Thursday, Friday, Saturday, Sunday & Bank Holiday Mondays 11am - 5pm.

Admission Rates: Adults £4.00, Senior Citizens £4.00, Child £1.00

Groups Rates: Reductions for groups over 10.

Facilities: Picnic Area, Plant Sales, Dogs on leads and Tea Rooms serving Hot & Cold Refreshments.

Disabled Access: Yes. Toilet and parking for disabled on site. Wheelchairs on loan.

Tours/Events: Guided Tours by Arrangement.

Coach Parking: Yes

Length of Visit: 2 hours to all day

Booking Contact: Nora Howells
Arley Arboretum, Arley Estate Office, Arley, Nr Bewdley, Worcs, DY12 1XG
Telephone: 01299 861868 or 01299 861368

Email: info@arley-arboretum.org.uk

Website: www.arley-arboretum.org.uk

Location: Off the A442 - Kidderminster/Bridgnorth/Telford Road - brown signed from Shatterford on A442.

Please quote this guide when booking

In 1751 the 6th Earl of Coventry commissioned Lancelot 'Capability' Brown to redesign his country seat of Croome. The project took over 30 years and established the principles of the "English Landscape Style" - an idealised vision of nature.

The gardens consist of winding shrubberies leading to ornate buildings designed by Adam and Wyatt. Brown also created an artificial lake, over a mile long. The wider parkland offers stunning views of 'eye-catcher' follies.

The park later slipped into decline, becoming reclaimed by nature. The National Trust acquired the park in 1996, and has now completed the first phase of restoration. Thousands of trees and shrubs have been replanted, the lake dredged, paths reinstated and garden buildings restored.

Croome, the first complete creation from one of England's greatest designers, gives visitors a unique opportunity to see a landscape in the making.

Fact File

Opening Times: 3rd March – 30th April + 6th September – 29th October Wednesday – Sunday + Bank Holiday Mondays 10am – 5.30pm; 1st May – 3rd September – Daily 10am – 5.30pm; 1st November – 17th December Wednesday – Sunday 10am – 4pm.

Admission Rates: Adults £3.90, Children £1.90. Family £9.50

Group Rates: Minimum Groups Size: 15 Adults: £3.30

Facilities: Ice creams and vending machine.

Disabled Access: Yes. Toilet and parking on site. Wheelchair Loan booking available.

Tours/Events: Guided tours available at £6.00 each. Full programme of events. Please call for information.

Coach Parking: Yes.

Length of Visit: 1 1/2 - 2 hours

Booking Contact Wendy Carter. Croome Park, NT Estate Office, Builders Yard, High Green, Severn Stoke, Worcestershire WR8 9JS
Telephone: 01905 371006 Fax: 01905 371090

Email: croomepark@nationaltrust.org.uk

Website: www.nationaltrust.org.uk

Location: 9 Miles south of Worcester. Signposted on A38 and B4004 from Pershore.

Please quote this guide when booking

This lovely 30 acre garden is owned by the Berkeley family, whose other home is historic 12th Century Berkeley Castle in Gloucestershire.

At Spetchley you will find most aspects of gardening, the formal and informal, woodland and herbaceous. A Garden full of secrets, every corner reveals some new vista, some new treasure of the plant world, whether it be tree, shrub or plant. The exuberant planting and the peaceful walks make this an oasis of peace and quiet. Many of the vast collection of plants are rarely found outside the major botanical gardens. The wonderful display of spring bulbs in April and May, together with flowering trees and shrubs, are followed in June and July by the large selection of roses, whilst July, August and September reveal the great herbaceous borders in all their glory. This is indeed a garden for all seasons.

Fact File

Opening Times:	21st March - 30th September. Wednesday - Sunday 11am - 6pm,
	1st - 31st March. Saturdays and Sundays 11am - 4pm.
	Bank Holiday Mondays 11am - 6pm. Closed all Saturdays and all other Mondays.
	Last admissions one hour before closing.
Admission Rates:	Adults £5.00, Senior Citizen £5.00, Under 16s free. Adults Season Tickets £25.00
Group Rates:	Minimum group size: 25
	Adults £4.50, Senior Citizen £4.50, Child £1.90.
Facilities:	Tea Room
Disabled Access:	Partial. Parking for disabled on site, Booking necessary for parties. (Access restricted, please telephone contact details below for advice).
Tours/Events:	Specialist Plant Fair 24th April 2005. Concert Sat 2nd July.
Coach Parking:	Yes.
Length of Visit:	2 hours minimum.
Booking Contact:	Berkeley Estate Office, Ham, Berkeley, Gloucestershire GL13 9QL.
	Tel: 01453 810303 Fax: 01453 511915
Email:	hb@spetchleygardens.co.uk
Website:	www.spetchleygardens.co.uk
Location:	2 miles east of Worcester on A44, leave M5 at either junctions 6 or 7

Please quote this guide when booking

Burton Agnes Hall & Gardens   Yorkshire

The Elizabethan Hall is surrounded by lawns and yew topiary bushes. To the east there is a classical pond with fountains and a newly constructed pebble mosaic. The old Elizabethan walled garden is accessed through a small gate and here you will find over 3,000 different plants. There is a potager filled with herbs and vegetables, herbaceous borders, a maze, fruit beds, a jungle garden with large leaved plants, grasses and bamboos planted in gravel, a campanula garden containing a national collection of campanulas, a giant knot garden with colour theme gardens divided by trellis and each containing a paved area forming a giant game board.

Fact File

Opening Times:	1st April – 31st October: 11.00 a.m. – 5.00 p.m.
Admission Rates:	Adults: £2.75, Senior Citizens: £2.50, Children: £1.30.
Facilities:	Shops, Plant Sales, Café.
Disabled Access:	Yes. Toilet and car parking on site. Wheelchair loan available please book.
Tours/Events:	Guided tours available. Introductory talks if requested for groups. Contact the booking office for details. Gardeners' fair 10th and 11th June 2006.
Coach Parking:	Yes
Length of Visit:	1 hour.
Booking Contact	Bridget Bramhall Burton Agnes Hall & Gardens, Burton Agnes, Driffield YO25 4NB. Telephone 01262 490324 Fax: 01262 490513
Email:	burton.agnes@farmline.com
Website:	www.burton-agnes.com
Location:	On A014 between Driffield and Bridlington.

Please quote this guide when booking

Fountains Abbey & Studley Royal Water Garden   Yorkshire

One of the most remarkable sites in Europe, sheltered in a secluded valley, Fountains Abbey and Studley Royal, a World Heritage Site, encompasses the spectacular remains of a 12th century Cistercian abbey with one of the finest surviving monastic watermills in Britain, an Elizabethan mansion, and one of the best surviving examples of a Georgian green water garden. Elegant ornamental lakes, avenues, temples and cascades provide a succession of unforgettable eye-catching vistas in an atmosphere of peace and tranquillity. St Mary's Church, built by William Burges in the 19th century, provides a dramatic focal point to the medieval Deer park with over 500 Deer.

Small museum near to the Abbey. Exhibitions in Fountains Hall, Swanley Grange and the Mill.

Fact File

Opening Times: March - October 10am - 5pm, November - February 10am - 4pm.
Closed Fridays in November - January and closed 24th and 25th December.

Admission Rates: Adults £6.50, Senior Citizen £6.50, Child £3.50, NT/EH Members Free, Family's £17.50.

Groups Rates: Group discounts and bespoke tours available, call the Group Visits Organiser on 01765 643197.

Facilities: Visitor Centre, Shop, Tea Room, Restaurant, Kiosk.

Disabled Access: Yes. Toilet and parking for disabled on site. Wheelchairs on loan, booking necessary.

Tours/Events: Guided Tours for groups, must be pre booked, telephone 01765 643197.
Annual events programme, please enqire for details.

Coach Parking: Yes

Length of Visit: 1 1/2 hours minimum.

Booking Contact: Fountains Abbey, Ripon, Yorkshire, HG4 3DY
Telephone: 01765 608888   Fax: 01765 601002

Email: fountainsenquiries@nationaltrust.org.uk

Website: www.fountainsabbey.org.uk   www.nationaltrust.org.uk

Location: 4 miles west of Ripon of B6265 to Pateley Bridge, signposted from A1, 10 miles north of Harrogate A61.

Please quote this guide when booking

RHS Garden Harlow Carr   North Yorkshire

Harlow Carr is the newest and most northerly of the four RHS gardens. This, along with its challenging growing conditions, offers an ideal place to view what can be grown successfully in the region.

The garden is seeing exciting new developments whilst retaining its truly tranquil and welcoming atmosphere. Probably the most spectacular are the dramatic new Long Borders that edge the path to 'Gardens Through Time'. Their use of mixed perennials, grasses and roses beautifully combines sustainable practice, inspirational horticulture and a contemporary twist! Also not to be missed are the stunning new Main Borders – a gorgeous mix of herbaceous perennials, grasses and shrubs, starting with hot vibrant colours and gradually moving to cooler shades towards the streamside.

The garden offers interest for all seasons – from vegetables to wildflowers, alpines to woodland – and now with the fabulous Bettys Garden Café offering delicious food and the best teas and coffees, it really is growing to inspire.

Fact File

Opening Times: 9.30am - 6pm (4pm Nov - Feb incl.) with last entry 1 hour before closing.

Admission Rates: Adults £6.00, Child (6-16yrs) £1.60 (under 6 Free).

Groups Rates: Minimum group size 10, Adults £4.60.

Facilities: Largest Gardening Bookshop in the north, Gift Shop, Bettys Cafe Tea Rooms, Plant Centre, Museum of Gardening.

Disabled Access: Yes. Toilet and parking for disabled on site. Wheelchairs on loan, booking necessary.

Tours/Events: A full programme of events is available from the gardens.

Coach Parking: Yes

Length of Visit: 1 - 2 hours

Booking Contact: Moira Malcolm
RHS Garden Harlow Carr, Crag Lane, Harrogate, HG3 1QB
Tel: 01423 565418 Fax: 01423 530663

Email: admin-harlowcarr@rhs.org.uk

Website: www.rhs.org.uk/harlowcarr

Location: Take the B6162 Otley Road out of Harrogate towards Beckwithshaw.
Harlow Carr is 1.5 miles on the right.

Please quote this guide when booking

Newby Hall was built between 1691-1695, shortly afterwards the owner, Sir Edward Blackett, commissioned Peter Aram to lay out formal gardens in keeping with the period. Very little of Aram's layout for Newby remains today and the present design is largely attributable to the present owner's grandfather, the late Major Edward Compton, who inherited in 1921. Influenced by Lawrence Johnston's Hidcote Manor in Gloucestershire, he created a main axis for the garden running from the south front of the house down to the River Ure. The axis consisted of double herbaceous borders flanked by yew hedges. Either side of the borders are numerous compartmented gardens such as the Rose Garden, the Autumn Garden, the Rock Garden, the Laburnum pergola walk, a Water Garden and even a Tropical Garden here in North Yorkshire - truly a 'Garden for all Seasons'. Newby also holds the National Collection of CORNUS.

Fact File

Opening Times:	1st April - 1st October, 11am - 5.30pm, Tuesday - Sunday & Bank Holidays, and Mondays in July and August.
Admission Rates:	(2005 Rates). Adults £6.70, Senior Citizen £5.70, Child £5.00.
Groups Rates:	Minimum group size 15
	Adults £5.70, Senior Citizen £5.70, Child £4.70
Facilities:	Visitor Centre, Shop, Plant Sales, Teas, Restaurant.
Disabled Access:	Yes. Toilet and parking for disabled on site. Wheelchairs on loan, booking necessary.
Tours/Events:	Tours on request with pre-booking essential.
Coach Parking:	Yes
Length of Visit:	2 hours minimum
Booking Contact:	Rosemary Triffit
	Newby Hall, Ripon, North Yorkshire, HG4 5AE
	Tel: 01423 322583 Fax: 01423 324452
Email:	info@newbyhall.com
Website:	www.newbyhall.com
Location:	2 miles from A1M at Ripon exit - junction 48.

Please quote this guide when booking

DERBYSHIRE'S BEST KEPT SECRET
(Just off Junction 30 of the M1)
Resplendent in acres of beautiful gardens and woodland sits Renishaw Hall, the family residence of the Sitwell family since the early 17th century.

The gardens, laid out over 100 years ago, consist of yew hedged 'rooms' filled with an impressive collection of plants. Rare trees, shrubs, roses, bulb, climbers and annuals are all combined for maximum aesthetic appeal.

Adjacent to the garden is an ancient Bluebell wood. In the recently created woodland garden is a Laburnham Tunnel, found alongside rhododendrons, camellias and magnolias.

See the National Collection of Yuccas and The Sculpture Park, featuring contemporary works.

Gardens, Museums and Galleries.
Gallery Café serving excellent food.
Full Calendar of Events.

Fact File

Opening Times:	Open March 30th to October 1st 10.30am - 4.30pm Thursday through to Sunday and Bank Holiday Mondays.
Admission Rates:	Adults: £5.00 (tbc), Senior Citizens: £4.20 (tbc), Children: Free under 10
Group Rates:	Minimum Groups Size: 25 (Hall tour) £9.95
Facilities:	Shop. Plant sales. Restaurant/teas
Disabled Access:	Yes. Toilet and car parking on site
Tours/Events:	Guided tours available.
Coach Parking:	Yes
Length of Visit:	Hall tour – $1^1/2$ hours
Booking Contact:	Cheryl Wallace, Angela Bywater Renishaw Hall Gardens, Renishaw Hall, Renishaw Park, Renishaw, Nr. Sheffield, S21 3WB. Telephone: 01246 432310 Fax: 01246 430760
Email:	Info2@renishaw-hall.co.uk
Website:	www.sltwell.co.uk
Location:	Junction 30 off the M1. A6135 to Sheffield/Eckington.

Please quote this guide when booking

Ripley Castle Gardens North Yorkshire

These substantial walled gardens and wooded pleasure grounds, recently restored and much improved, are well worth visiting in all seasons: massive herbaceous borders, Victorian Kitchen garden with rare vegetable collection, the National Hyacinth Collection, herb and shade borders, extensive hothouses and thousands of snowdrops, bluebells, daffodils and narcissi. A stroll around the lake takes you through the deer park, where fallow deer graze beneath the boughs of living oak trees, now believed to be over a thousand years old. This walk also offers the best views of the 14th century castle.

Guided tours of the castle give you a chance to view the civil war armour, secret priests hiding hole and splendid furnishings. On site facilities include ample free parking, wc's (including disabled), tea room, historic inn with beer garden and gift shop selling plants.

Fact File

Opening Times:	Daily - Throughout the year 9am - 5pm (dusk in the winter months).
Admission Rates:	Adults £4.00, Senior Citizen £3.50, Child £2.50. (under 5 yrs Free)
Groups Rates:	Minimum group size 15 people
	Adults £3.50, Senior Citizen £3.50, Child £2.50.
Facilities:	Gift Shop, Plant Sales, Tea Rooms, Restaurant, Children's play area.
Disabled Access:	Yes. Toilet and parking for diabled on site. Wheelchairs on loan, booking necessary.
Tours/Events:	Guided tours of gardens by prior arrangement only.
Coach Parking:	Yes
Booking Contact:	Anneliesse Ford
	Ripley Castle Gardens, Ripley, Nr Harrogate, North Yorkshire, HG3 3AY
	Telephone: 01423 770152 Fax: 01423 771745
Email:	groups@ripleycastle.co.uk
Website:	www.ripleycastle.co.uk
Location:	Three miles north of Harrogate on the A61.

Please quote this guide when booking

Scotland

" The quality of light surpasses all other places...

as the mist lessens the loch glistens whilst the gorse and

heather burst into flame. Even the funereal peat softens, as if in

response to the deepening red of the pine".

'On the Western Isle' E.B. Hamilton

Scottish gardens are unique. They may contain (in some instances) similar plants

and architecture to their English cousins but there the similarity ends. The rich acid soils,

abundance of water and clarity of air combine to create plants of great vigour and stunning

vistas - both within the garden and to the borrowed landscape beyond. From Castle Kennedy

in the south to Armadale Castle on the Isle of Skye this book provides a choice selection

of Scotland's finest gardens.

Armadale Castle Gardens & Museum of the Isles   Isle of Skye

Armadale Castle Gardens & Museum of the Isles has a spectacular setting within the Sleat Peninsula of the Isle of Skye called the 'Garden of Skye'.

The forty acre Garden is set around the ruins of Armadale Castle. The warm, generally frost free climate of the west coast of Scotland - a result of the Gulf Stream - allows these sheltered gardens, dating back to the 17th Century, to flourish.

Wander over the expanses of lawn leading from the ruined Armadale Castle to viewpoints overlooking the hills of Knoydart. Terraced walks and landscaped ponds contrasting with wildflower meadows bring the natural and formal side by side. The Nature Trails provide another dimension to this garden experience. In May during the bluebell season, a carpet of blue around the Arboretum creates a visual and fragrance sensation that is so prevalent around the gardens at that time of year.

Fact File

Opening Times: 9.30am - 5.00pm (last entry 5pm), 7 days April to October (incl).
Admission Rates: Adults £4.90, Senior Citizen £3.80, Child £3.50, Family £14.00.
Groups Rates: Minimum group size: 8
Adults £3.40, Senior Citizen £3.20, Child £3.20.
Facilities: 40 Acres of Woodland Garden and mature Trails, Museum of the Isles, Restaurant, 3 Shops.
Disabled Access: Yes, Toilet and Parking for disabled on site. Electric Wheelchairs on loan, booking necessary.
Tours/Events: Guided walks on request.
Coach Parking: Yes
Length of Visit: 2 hours
Booking Contact: Mags MacDonald
Armadale Castle, Armadale, Sleat, Isle of Skye, IV45 8RS
Telephone: 01471 844305 Fax: 01471 844275
Email: office@clandonald.com
Website: www.clandonald.com
Location: 2 minutes from Armadale/Mallaig Ferry. 20 miles from Skyebridge on A851.

Please quote this guide when booking

Castle Kennedy Gardens

A beautiful landscaped garden extending to 75 acres set between two large freshwater lochs. The gardens are famous for their collection of trees and rhododendrons from around the world.

The grounds were extensively landscaped in the 18th century. laid out with terraces and avenues. The plant collections include specimens provided by Joseph Hooker and probably the oldest avenue of Monkey Puzzle trees.

Fact File

Opening Times:	1st April - 30th September, seven days a week, 10am- 5pm.
Admission Rates:	Adults £4.00, Senior Citizen £3.00, Child £1.00
Groups Rates:	Minimum group size 20 10% discount on normal admission rates.
Facilities:	Tea Shop, Plant sales.
Disabled Access:	Limited. toilet and parking for disabled on site.
Tours/Events:	None.
Coach Parking:	Yes
Length of Visit:	1 - 4 hours
Booking Contact:	Castle Kennedy Gardens, Stair Estates, Rephad, Stanraer, Dumfries & Galloway, DG9 8BX Gardens Tel: 01581 400225 Telephone: 01776 702024 Fax: 01776 706248
Email:	info@castlekennedygardens.co.uk
Website:	www.castlekennedygardens.co.uk
Location:	Approximately 5 miles east of Stranraer on A75.

Please quote this guide when booking

Cawdor Castle, the most romantic Castle in the Highlands, dating from the 14th century is fortunate to have 3 gardens: the walled garden is the oldest and dates from circa 1600. It was planted in 1981 with a series of symbolic gardens: a holly maze that depicts the Minotour's Labyrinth at Knossos in Crete; a Paradise Garden, where the sound of water and the smell of flowers create peace; a Knot Garden, whose plants were used for medicinal, culinary or still room preparations in the Middle Ages; and a Garden of Eden planted with old Scottish apple trees. The flower garden, south of the Castle, was laid out in the 18th century with rose beds edged with lavender, great herbaceous borders– yet there is still a family feel and plants are chosen out of affection, not affectation. The Auchindoune Garden, which is open on Tuesdays and Thursdays in May, June and July or by appointment, has an organic vegetable garden growing a variety of heritage vegetables; and a Tibetan Garden along the banks of the burn, which was planted with specimens brought back by Jack Cawdor from his travels with Kingdon Ward to the Tsangpo Gorges in 1924.

Fact File

Opening Times: 1st May to 8th October, 10.30 a.m to 5.30 pm, last admission 5pm.

Admission Rates: Castle, garden and grounds – Adult £7.00, OAP £6.00 Gardens and grounds only - £3.70
Auchindoune Gardens - £3.00

Group Rates: Minimum Groups Size: 20
Castle, gardens and grounds - £6.10 Gardens and grounds only - £3.70

Facilities: Three beautiful gardens, nature trails, 9 hole golf course, putting green, gift shop, book shop, & wool shop, restaurant and snack bar.

Disabled Access: Access to gardens, grounds, restaurant, shops and toilet facilities. Access to castle limited.

Tours/Events: Guided tours of gardens by Head Gardener by arrangement. Special Gardens Weekend – 3rd & 4th June 2006. RHS lecture 'Plant Magic' by Sue Hoy – Saturday 24th June at 11am in Cawdor Village Hall (booking necessary).

Coach Parking: Yes.

Length of Visit: Approximately 2 hours.

Booking Contact Secretary, Cawdor Castle and Gardens, Nairn, IV12 5RD
Telephone: 01667 404401 Fax: 01667 404674

Email: info@cawdorcastle.com

Website: www.cawdorcastle.com

Location: Situated between Inverness (15 miles) and Nairn (5 miles) on the B9090 off the A96.

Please quote this guide when booking

Hercules Garden & Blair Castle Perthshire

Hercules Garden is a walled garden of ten acres, over looked by a fine statue of Hercules by John Cheere, placed on a rise in a shrub walk running east from Blair Castle, the ancestral home of the Dukes of Atholl. It was the 2nd Duke who landscaped the grounds in the mid 18th century, his scheme evolved to create two ponds in a large walled garden designed in the 'Ferme Ornee' manner-fruit and vegetables grown among ornamental planting schemes and sweet smelling shrubs.

Today the garden contains a large collection of fruit trees, a terrace over 300 meters long flanked by herbaceous borders, a variety of beds for vegetables, herbs, cut flowers, shade loving plants, roses and annuals. The layout is based on the 2nd Duke's design and includes some of the original, heather thatched huts for the nesting birds and a restored folly, housing a display about the restoration of the garden.

Fact File

Opening Times:	9.30am - 4.30pm last entry.
Admission Rates:	Grounds & Garden: Adults £2.30, Senior Citizen £2.30, Children £1.20.
Group Rates:	Minimum group size: 12. Adults £2.10, Senior Citizen £2.10, Children £1.10.
Facilities:	Shop, Teas, Restaurant, Castle (5 Star historic Home).
Disabled Access:	Yes. Toilet & parking for disabled on site. Wheelchairs on loan, booking necessary.
Tours/Events:	Please Call For details or visit website.
Coach Parking:	Yes
Length of Visit:	Approx 2 hours
Booking Contact:	Admin Office
	Blair Castle, Blair Atholl, Pitlochry, Perthshire PH18 5TL
	Telephone 01796 481207 Fax: 01796 481487
Email:	office@blair-castle.co.uk
Website:	www.blair-castle.co.uk
Location:	Off A9 Blair Atholl on Perth/Inverness Road (35mins Perth). 1 1/2 hours Edinburgh.

Please quote this guide when booking

Torosay Castle, completed in 1858 in the Scottish Baronial style by the eminent architect David Bryce, is one of the finer examples of his work, resulting in a combination of elegance and informality, grandeur and homeliness.

A unique combination of formal terraces and dramatic West Highland scenery makes Torosay a spectacular setting, which, together with a mild climate results in superb specimens of rare, unusual and beautiful plants.

A large collection of Statuary and many niche gardens makes Torosay a joy to explore and provides many peaceful corners in which to relax.

Fact File

Opening Times:	House: 1st April - 31st October, 10.30am - 5.00pm.
	Gardens: Open all year, 9.00am - 7.00pm.
Admission Rates:	Adults £5.50, Concessions £5.00, Child £2.25.
Group Rates:	Minimum group size: 10
	Adults £5.00, Concessions £5.00, Child £2.00.
Facilities:	Shop, Plant Sales, Children's Play Area, Tea Room, Holiday Cottages, Parking on site.
Disabled Access:	Yes to gardens only. Toilet and parking for disabled on site.
Tours/Events:	Tours available to groups by arrangement at a cost of £7 per person.
	Concerts, plays etc advertised seperately.
Coach Parking:	Yes
Length of Visit:	2 hours minimum.
Booking Contact:	Mr James/Carol Casey.
	Torosay Castle, Craignure, Isle of Mull PA65 6AY
	Telephone: 01680 812421 Fax: 01680 812470
Email:	info@torosay.com
Website:	www.torosay.com
Location:	1 1/2 miles from Craignure (ferry terminal) on A849/on foot by forest walk or by narrow gauge railway.

Please quote this guide when booking

Wales

" It is warming indeed to see the avenues that I then planted growing

so flourishingly and the whole place maturing in ever increasing beauty".

Clough Williams-Ellis

From Cardiff Bay to the mountains of Snowdonia, Wales is a country of contrasts.

This is clearly portrayed by the gardens in this book. Here you will find gardens

of yesterday and gardens of tomorrow. From the fifteenth century beginnings of Aberglasney

to the twenty-first century steel and glass structures of Middleton,

there are inspirational gardens in Wales for us all to enjoy.

Aberglasney Gardens

Carmarthenshire

Aberglasney is one of the Country's most exciting garden restoration projects. The Gardens have wonderful horticultural qualities and a mysterious history. Within the nine acres of garden are six different garden spaces including three walled gardens. At its heart is a unique and fully restored Elizabethan/ Jacobean cloister garden and a parapet walk, which is the only example that survived in the UK. The Garden contains a magnificent collection of rare and unusual plants which are seldom seen elsewhere in the country.

The House and Garden will continually be improved over the years, the result will be a world renowned Garden set in the beautiful landscape of the Tywi Valley. There is a Café in the grounds, which serves delectable light lunches and snacks. In the summer, tea can be taken on the terrace overlooking the Pool Garden. There is also a shop and plant sales area.

The creation of a winter garden in 2005 called the Ninfarium (after the mediaeval garden near Rome) is situated in the ruinous central courtyard of the mansion. This provides a totally unique garden environment, displaying a wonderful range of exotic sub-tropical plants.

Fact File

Opening Times: Summer: 10am - 6pm (last entry at 5pm).
Winter: 10.30am - 4pm.
Admission Rates: Adults £6.00, Senior Citizen £5.00, Child £3.00
Groups Rates: Minimum group size 10
Adults £5.50, Senior Citizen £4.50, Child £3.00
Facilities: Shop, Plant Sales, Cafe.
Disabled Access: Yes. Toilet and parking for disabled on site. Wheelchairs on loan, booking necessary.
Tours/Events: Guided tours on request.
Coach Parking: Yes
Length of Visit: 2 - 4 hours
Booking Contact: Bookings Department.
Aberglasney Gardens, Llangathen, Carmarthenshire, SA32 8QH
Telephone: 01558 668998   Fax: 01558 668998
Email: info@aberglasney.org.uk
Website: www.aberglasney.org
Location: Four miles outside Llandeilo of the A40.

Please quote this guide when booking

Bodnant Garden is one of the finest gardens in the country not only known for its magnificent collections of rhododendrons, camellias and magnolias but also for its idyllic setting above the River Conwy with extensive views of the Snowdonia range.

Visit in early Spring (March and April) and be rewarded by the sight of carpets of golden daffodils and other spring bulbs, as well as the beautiful blooms of the magnolias, camellias and flowering cherries. The spectacular rhododendrons and azaleas will delight from mid April until late May, whilst the famous original Laburnum Arch is an overwhelming mass of yellow blooms from mid-may to mid-June. The herbaceous borders, roses, hydrangeos, clematis and water liles flower from the middle of June until September.

All these, together with the outstanding October autumn colours make Bodnant truly a garden offering interest for all the seasons.

Fact File

Opening Times: 11th March - 5th Nov 2006
Admission Rates: Adults £6.00, Child £3.00 (5-16yrs)
Groups Rates: Minimum group size 20.
                        Adults £5.00, Child £3.00.
Facilities: Tearoom, Car & Coach Park, Plant & Gift Centre.
Disabled Access: Yes. Toilet and parking for disabled on site. Wheelchairs on loan.
Tours/Events: Phone for details
Coach Parking: Yes
Length of Visit: 2 hours +
Booking Contact: Ann Harvey
                        Bodnant Garden, Tal Y cafn, Nr Colwyn Bay, Conwy. LL28 5RE
                        Telephone: 01492 650460 Fax: 01492 650448
Email: office@bodnantgarden.co.uk
Website: www.bodnantgarden.co.uk
Location: 8 miles south of Llandudno and Colwyn Bay just off A470, signposted from the A55, exit at junction 19.

Please quote this guide when booking

Dyffryn Gardens   Vale of Glamorgan

Set in the heart of the Vale of Glamorgan countryside, this exceptional example of Edwardian garden design is currently being restored with assistance from the Heritage Lottery Fund. Designed by Thomas Mawson for the avid plant collector Reginald Cory, this unique collaboration has resulted in splendid Great Lawns, intimate garden rooms and an arboretum of rare and unusual trees from around the world.

Throughout the restoration the gardens remain open to the public with only sections of the 55 acres of designed landscape closed during the works. Restoration completed in recent years include the Pompeiian Garden, Herbaceous Border, Panel Garden, Reflecting Pool, Heather Garden and Fernery.

Ongoing works are focusing on improving access for all visitors, the glasshouse and Walled Kitchen Garden. Enjoy a relaxing stroll or come and see one of the many events taking place throught the summer.

Fact File

Opening Times: 1st April to September 10am - 6pm, October 10am - 5pm
(Closed November - March for restoration work)

Admission Rates: Adults £3.50, Family (2 Adults & 2 Conc.) £7.00, Conc. £2.50, Disabled £2.00, Carers Free.

Groups Rates: Minimum group size: 15 - Adults £3.00

Facilities: Visitor Centre, Shop, Tea Room, Plant Sales.

Disabled Access: Yes. Toilet and parking for disabled on site. Wheelchairs on loan, booking preferable.

Tours/Events: Tours monthly with Head Gardener no additional charge, by arrangement - Charge £1 PP.
Varied programme of events from Easter to October.

Coach Parking: Yes

Length of Visit: 2 - 3 hours

Booking Contact: Mrs Deborah Kerslake
Dyffryn Gardens, St Nicholas, Vale of Glamorgan, CF5 6SU
Telephone: 029 20593328   Fax: 029 20591966

Email: DKerslake@valeofglamorgan.gov.uk

Website: www.dyffryngardens.org.uk

Location: Exit M4 at J33 to A4232 (signposted Barry). At roundabout take 1st exit (A4232). At junction with A48/A4050 exit the A4232 at Culverhouse Cross - Take 4th exit A48 (signposted Cowbridge). Turn left at lights in St Nicholas Village. Dyffryn is on right one and a half miles.

Please quote this guide when booking

Glansevern Hall was built, in Greek Revival style, by Sir Arthur Davies Owen at the turn of the 18th/19th Century.

It looks down on the River Severn from an enclosure of gardens set in wider parkland. Near the house are fine lawns studded with herbaceous and rose beds and a wide border backed by brick walls. A Victorian orangery and a large fountain face each other across the lawns. The large walled garden has been ingeniously divided into compartments separated by hornbeam hedges and ornamental ironwork. There is a rock garden of exceptional size, built of limestone and tufa, which creates a walk-through grotto. A litlle further afield, woodland walks are laid out around the 4 acre lake and pass through a water garden which, especially in May and June, presents a riot of growth and colour.

Glanservern is noted for its collection of unusual trees.

Fact File

Opening Times:	Easter Friday, Saturday and Monday 14th, 15th and 17th April. Thereafter every Thursday, Friday, Saturday and Bank Holiday Monday 12.00 noon - 5.00 pm until 30th September. Group on any other day, booking necessary.
Admission Rates:	Adults £3.50, Senior Citizen £3.00, Child Free
Facilities:	Tea Room & Light Lunches (all Homemade), Plant Sales, Art Gallery.
Disabled Access:	Yes. Toilet and parking for disabled on site.
Tours/Events:	Guided walk indentifying the large number of unusual trees.
Coach Parking:	Yes
Length of Visit:	1 1/2 hours
Booking Contact:	Neville Thomas Glanservern Hall Gardens, Berriew, Welshpool, Powys, SY21 8AH Telephone: 01686 640200 Fax: 01686 640829
Email:	glansevern@ukonline.co.uk
Website:	www.glansevern.co.uk
Location:	Signposted at Berriew on A483 between Welshpool and Newtown, North Powys, 4 miles S W of Powys Castle.

This remarkable botanic garden is blossoming into one of the most beautiful and stimulating gardens in the UK. Like all young things its unique character develops every year, offering an unrivalled chance to see an international gem in the making. Nestled in the stunning beautiful Tywi Valley its 568 acres of lovely themed gardens, rolling regency parkland and secluded woodlands are an inspired blend of the past and future. The awe-inspiring Great Glasshouse houses a unique collection of Mediterranean plants from around the world which are carefully conserved and displayed. The recently restored double-walled garden is brimming with dazzling displays. Many other delights include Europe's largest herbaceous border, Japanese, Genetic and Physic gardens, Auricula theatre, restored lakes, cascades and other water features, interactive exhibitions including a 19th century restored apothecary and 360˚ multimedia theatre, children's activities, mini farm and adventure playground and so much more. Add this to a restaurant, shop and plant centre and you have a perfect day out for all the family.

Fact File

Opening Times: 10am - 6pm British summer time. 10am - 4.30pm British winter time. (Closed Christmas Day).

Admission Rates: Adults £7.50, Senior Citizen £5.50, Child £2.50 (5-15)
Family (2 adults, 4 children) £17.00, Under 5's free.

Groups Rates: Minimum group size 10
Adults £6.50, Senior Citizen £4.50, Child £2.00

Facilities: Visitor Centre, Shop, Restaurant, Cafe, Plant Centre, 360 degrees Multimedia Theatre, Conference Centre, Children's Activity Centre.

Disabled Access: Yes. Toilets and parking for disabled on site. Wheelchair and motorised scooters on loan, booking necessary.

Tours/Events: Daily guided tours. Full events programme.

Coach Parking: Yes

Length of Visit: 4 hours

Booking Contact: The National Botanic Garden of Wales, Llanarthne, Carmarthenshire, SA32 8HG.
Telephone: 01558 668768   Fax: 01558 668933

Email: info@gardenofwales.org.uk

Website: www.gardenofwales.org.uk

Location: About an hours drive from Cardiff, two hours drive from Bristol. Just off the A48, which links directly to the M4 and onto the M5.

Please quote this guide when booking

If you would like to order additional copies of Gardens to Visit 2006
Please contact the address below

Thanks go to the Gardens and Garden Visitors who have provided feedback on the information
they would like to see within this publication.

ISBN 0-9551833-0-8

ISBN 978-0-9551833-0-0

Gardens to Visit 2006 is specially published by
Publicity Works
P.O. Box 32
Tetbury
Gloucestershire
GL8 8BF
Telephone: 01453 836730 Fax: 01453 835285
Email: mail@publicity-works.org

Index

The Italianate village of Portmeirion is surrounded by 70 acres of sub-tropical woodlands known as *Y Gwyllt* ("the wild place"- it was once an area of rough pasture and gorse) with its Victorian shelters, temples and dogs' cemetery. From the 1840s successive tenants landscaped and planted the area with a variety of native and exotic trees. From the early 1900s the Gwyllt was developed by Caton Haig as an exotic woodland garden until his death in 1941 when the garden was bought by Clough Williams-Ellis and incorporated into his Portmeirion estate.

A tree trail has recently been established giving access to some of the most important trees in the garden including one hundred year old rhododendrons, gigantic Californian coast redwoods, the papauma or New Zealand 'dancing tree', the UK's largest Japanese cedar 'elegans' and tallest Chilean maiten tree, the ginkgo or maidenhair tree and many others.

Fact File

Opening Times:	All Year 9.30 - 17.30
Admission Rates:	Adult £6.50, Senior Citizen £5.00, Child £3.50 Family (2+2) £16.00
Group Rates:	Minimum group size: 12
	Adult £4.80, Senior Citizen £4.00, Child £2.40
Facilities:	Gift Shop, Plant Sales, Teas, Restaurant, Audio Visual, Hotel, 7 Shops, Tree Trail, Beach.
Disabled Access:	Yes. Toilet and parking for disabled on site. Wheelchair on loan, booking advisable.
Tours/Events:	None
Coach Parking:	Yes
Length of Visit:	3 hours
Booking Contact:	Terry Williams. Toll Gate Manager
	Portmerion, Gwynedd, LL48 6ET.
	Telephone: 01766 772311 Fax: 01766 771331
Email:	info@portmeirion-village.com
Website:	www.portmeirion-village.com
Location:	Signposted off A487 at Minffordd between Penrhyndeudraeth and Porthmadog.

Please quote this guide when booking